1. Vatican II Revisited

Vatican II Revisited

Vatican II Revisited
Reflections By One Who Was There

Most Reverend Aloysius J Wycislo

ALBA · HOUSE NEW · YORK

Library of Congress Cataloging-in-Publication Data

Wycislo, Aloysius J.
      Vatican II revisited : reflections by one who was there / Aloysius
J. Wycislo.
            p. xiv + 184   cm.14 × 21.
      Bibliography: p.
      ISBN 0-8189-0522-0
      1. Vatican Council (2nd : 1962-1965)   2. Catholic Church —
Doctrines — History — 20th century.   3. Wycislo, Aloysius J.
I.   Title.
BX830   1962.W92   1987
262'.52 — dc 19   87-21325
                                                                  CIP

Designed, printed and bound in the United States of
America by the Fathers and Brothers of the
Society of St. Paul, 2187 Victory Boulevard,
Staten Island, New York 10314, as part of their
communications apostolate.

2 3 4 5 6 7 8 9 (Current Printing: first digit)

Dedication

In the last few years it has become evident that more and more of those who shared in the events of the Second Vatican Council are aging, retired or dead. A new generation of bishops who did not attend the Council have assumed positions of leadership. Young theologians have only teenage recollections of the Council itself and there are others who have only the fuzziest ideas about the shape of the Church before Vatican II. Perhaps this book will encourage them to dig back into that interesting history.

This book is dedicated to Albert Cardinal Meyer, Archbishop of Chicago, who, prior to his death in April 1965, opened for me the riches of his mind during the first three sessions of Vatican Council II that we lived together in Rome.

And, to the clergy, religious and laity of the Diocese of Green Bay, who cooperated with me as their shepherd, in giving effect in our local Church to the documents of the Council.

Contents

Introduction ix

   I.   Why The Council? 3

  II. The Bishops Come To Rome 13

 III. The Role Of The Theologians 25

 IV. Significant Speakers 41

   V. The New Image Of The Church 49

 VI. Word And Sacrament 65

 VII. Ministry 83

VIII. Ecumenism 103

 IX. The Theology Of Liberty 125

  X. The Church And The World 141

 XI. Hope For The Future 165

Bibliography 183

Name Index 185

This book is for those who were not there at the Rome of Vatican II, and for those who were born into a Church of change, of the future, of "The People of God" reflecting the life and ministry of the baptized in Christ.

Since December 8, 1965, when the Second Vatican Council concluded, a new generation has moved into membership in the Catholic Church that may or may not be familiar with the Council's prophetic teachings that now affect their lives.

This book tries to provide some answers to the why of Vatican Council II, something of its inner workings, and a history in the perspective of one who was there.

Very few bishops invited to Rome by Pope John XXIII on October 11, 1962, for the opening of the Second Vatican Council could have foreseen the historic crossroad they encountered and turned into that fateful day. In fact, one could surmise that most bishops may not have fully realized the impact of their participation until sometime after they resettled themselves back home into the routine of their work and began to implement the documents of Vatican II.

It is part of our Catholic tradition that the Church is guided by the Holy Spirit. It soon became the conviction of the bishops of Vatican II, now looking back on their work, that the Spirit indeed was a factor in their deliberations. From the earliest days of the Church, the decisions of Councils have played a definitive part in providing signposts along the road to salvation. In Councils (and especially in the Second Vatican Council), bishops, the leaders of their local Churches, in consort with the Pope, the Bishop of Rome and Pastor of the Universal Church, freely debated and reached conclusions in collegial responsibility, assisted by "periti" or experts in Scripture, theology, liturgy and the other Church sciences.

The Second Vatican Council showed us the magisterium (the principal teaching arm of the Church) in action. This very open Council, as will be evident in the chapters that follow, was an experience in discussion and debate (more politely called interventions), in criticism and in the revision of attitudes. As was evident, movements which had been under way for fifty years or more — liturgical, biblical, ecumenical — all surfaced on the floor of St. Peter's Basilica and were incorporated into the formal documents of the Council, to the surprise of many of the scholars involved in those movements.

Theologians and biblical scholars who had been "under a cloud" for years, surfaced as periti, and their post-Vatican II books and commentaries became popular reading. Chapter III tries to recapture a bit of their lives and the contributions they made to the deliberations of the Council.

The Council's insights and suggestions (Pope John XXIII insisted that Vatican II be a pastoral and not a doctrinal Council) are today pretty much a way of life, especially in the worship practices of the faithful. The interpretation and reading of the Bible has taken on new meaning and interest as the result of four years' work on the Dogmatic Constitution on Divine Revelation. The ecumenical movement however, may have bogged down because of the concern that the post-conciliar Church was aping Protestantism too much.

Another force that directly affected the administrative arm of the Church is the concept of collegiality, the sharing of responsibility that was so graphically emphasized in the Dogmatic Constitution on the Church. The successor of St. Peter, the Pope, is now seen as the head of the apostolic college of all the bishops. And that concept has come down (after all, we are still a hierarchical Church) to the very interested and involved Catholic in the pew. He now shares with his pastor responsibility for the goals and mission of his parish; or as a parish representative, shares with his bishop responsibility for the local or diocesan Church.

The philosophy behind the writing of this book is based on the conviction that by "looking back we may be able to see farther ahead." The problems that provoked Pope John XXIII to convene a General Council of the Church have not been swept away by Vatican II. But there is no point, as Winston Churchill said after the loss of Dunkirk during World War II, "to set up a quarrel between the past and the present, lest we face the danger of losing the future."

The future of the Church is everyone's concern. There is a bright future ahead if there is patience with change. We may be able to learn something from the mistakes of the past, as we are today learning how deep and wide is our varied Catholic tradition. There are unanswered questions: what language to use at Mass; the role of penance in our lives; what methods of birth control are open to Catholics; whether priests should marry; should women be ordained, etc. But these, and other questions were faced by the bishops of Vatican II and they tried to face up to most of them in the documents they gave the Universal Church.

The Pastoral Constitution on the Church in the Modern World, for instance, is in many ways an unfinished work. The elements of its teaching still need to find answers for the basic questions: what is the priesthood, family life, human culture, life in its economic, social and political dimensions? What is the stability of those elements in a society that faces the possibility of nuclear disaster, and has yet far to go in the building up of a family of nations?

We are all part of this new stage in human history, and the Church is a vital part of it. Vatican II's Pastoral Constitution on the Church in the Modern World raises the hope that there can develop a communion of persons, spearheaded by those who believe in Christ and are willing to be led by "the Holy Spirit in their journey to the kingdom of their Father" (#1).

Questions that were raised prior to Vatican II are being raised by another generation today that fails to see that the "old" applies to them too and that change needs the test of time. The "world" Pope John and his bishops were thinking about at Vatican II was the human race in its struggle to bring about true brotherhood, justice and peace for all of mankind. For the Church that meant looking at the Council as one great teacher providing guidelines on social issues long ago emphasized by Pope Leo XIII in *Rerum Novarum* and Pope John XXIII in *Mater et Magistra* and *Pacem in Terris*.

The inspiration for embarking on this book came as a result of a series of lectures on the Second Vatican Council and in a special way the encouragement of many priest alumni of St. Francis Seminary in Milwaukee, Wisconsin, where I provided a rather substantial review of the Council and something of Cardinal Meyer's participation in its proceedings. The Cardinal — once rector of that seminary, and later the Archbishop of Chicago, under whom the author served as Auxiliary Bishop — became one of the outstanding leaders and contributors to the Council agenda.

An added reason for writing this book comes of what Pope John Paul II stated "is a need for a bishop who took part in the Second Vatican Council to acquit himself of a debt." My sense of that debt is linked to a further response of the faith that was enhanced as a result of my participation in the Council. But really, my basic reason is to get you, the reader, to study the fascinating documents of the Second Vatican Council.

I am indebted to many who have encouraged me to share my insights of Vatican II, but in a special way I want to express my gratitude to the many sources that make up a good part of this book: the interventions made in the Council and the books and commentaries that have guided me.

I am grateful to Father Gordon Gilsdorf, the Censor Librorum for the Diocese of Green Bay, for his criticisms and suggestions; Father Robert Kabat, a young priest associated with us in the Marriage Tribunal of the Diocese, on whom I tested the contents of this book. And, of course, I am thankful to the staff of that Tribunal for their patience and consideration when I sometimes "tied up" the computer/printer in the office in which they gave me hospitality.

Vatican II Revisited

I.

Why The Council?

October 11, 1962, was a typical fall day in Rome, and the opening of the Ecumenical Council of Vatican II was in keeping with the Roman sense of what a great event should be all about. Cardinals, patriarchs, archbishops, bishops, abbots, priests, scholars and observers of non-Catholic denominations, from all parts of the world, converged on St. Peter's Basilica for what was a protracted opening ceremony of an event that would have lasting impact for generations to come.

Pope John XXIII stepped down from his gestatorial chair at the entrance to St. Peter's that eventful day and walked the center aisle of Christendom's greatest church, bowing and waving to his fellow bishops. The latter were cramped into two long rows of stalls, made up of a folding writing desk, a kneeler and a hard seat and back. Dressed in ceremonial purple, white copes and mitres, the world's bishops, just a few days arrived by ship, train and airplane, were soon engulfed in an atmosphere of status — little realizing the dynamic change that would affect their lives and the lives of the faithful they were called to serve. They came representing an essentially clerical Church, a Church that had set herself apart from the world. But that Church would in the next four years allow history, those "signs of the times," to invade every aspect of her life. They would be partners in modernizing some of her structures, simplifying the liturgy and even secularizing many of her symbols.

Yet, it took just a few weeks for them to learn the meaning of "aggiornamento," the word Pope John first used when he announced the idea of convening an Ecumenical Council. An Italian word which means "bringing up to date," it was to become for them and their flocks as familiar as "Hello" and "Good-bye."

The 737 bishops who were present for the First Vatican Council (1869-1870) came mostly from Europe. There were 48 archbishops and bishops and one abbot from the United States. On the other hand, the 2908 prelates who attended the four sessions of Vatican II (October 1962-December 1965) came from every part of the world. It was the largest of the Ecumenical Councils and it produced sixteen completed documents that have had and will have a profound effect upon the Church and her membership for a long time to come. There were 247 cardinals, archbishops and bishops from the United States, one abbot and a large number of non-Catholic observers as well as "periti" or scholars. These last assisted their bishops in the preparation of written and oral interventions before and during the Council. The American presence was also made significant through the establishment of the United States Press Panel, which was a source of daily news releases. These gave the sessions of Vatican II the greatest coverage ever accorded a religious meeting or a Council.

In essence Vatican II was a Council of the Universal Catholic Church, a Church no longer dominated by West-European tradition. It is not so much a Church looking in on herself, but a Church of the "People of God" reflecting the life and ministry of all those baptized in Christ.

After Pope John XXIII announced the Council, he wrote to all the bishops in the world and consulted them about the agenda. In addition, he consulted some eight hundred theologians. After that the Pope directed the Curia to begin the setting up of preparatory commissions which would study and develop the thousands of pages of suggestions that came from the bishops and the theologians.

However (and this is how Vatican II differed very radically from other Councils), the bishops, once they got their feet on the ground in Rome, changed the content of many of the schemata that were submitted to them during the sessions, reversed the order of their treatment or eliminated some proposals altogether.

For instance, the treatment of the place of the Blessed Virgin Mary in the life and work of the Church was not put into a separate document as some bishops wanted. Rather, it was made a separate chapter in the Dogmatic Constitution on the Church with the conviction that, after all, she too was a member of the people of God. The treatment of religious freedom (a much debated topic of special interest to the Anglo-Saxon nations), was first presented as a section of the Decree on Ecumenism by the Commission for Christian Unity. It became a separate document of its own (the Declaration on Religious Freedom). This was later labeled as THE American document of Vatican II.

Perhaps the most telling difference between Vatican I and Vatican II is the way in which the Council Fathers handled certain agenda items. In the case of Vatican I when it became clear that the controversial doctrine of papal infallibility would get through, some sixty bishops decided to go home rather than vote in favor of the doctrine. During a number of the sessions of Vatican II the bishops ''stuck it out'' in controversy. As a result, as will be shown later, controversial documents, like the ones on Revelation, Religious Freedom and others did not make the disappointed bishops leave for home.

By the way, the famous Schema 13, which later became the Pastoral Constitution on the Church in the Modern World, came from the conciliar floor of the aula in St. Peter's.

There were differences, too, in the way that membership to the various preparatory commissions came about.

At Vatican I the Roman Curia dominated to the point that of 96 consultors, or members, 61 were Italians living in Rome. At

Vatican II the commissions were made up of cardinals, bishops and scholars from every part of the world. But more of that later.

Finally, it must be noted that the Franco-Prussian War which erupted in July 1870 brought an end to Vatican Council I. Much of its unfinished business was left to the Second Vatican Council — matters like the bishops' collegial relationship to the Pope (so much related to the controversy over papal infallibility), the questions of ecumenism, the role of the laity in the Church, and the unfinished document on the Constitution on the Church.

How and why did the Second Vatican Council gather such momentum? The simplest answer goes back to the years between Vatican I and Vatican II. But then again as in the past history of the Church, the right Pope came along at the right time. As Pope John saw it, the time was ripe; as he so often put it, he had been reading and studying the "signs of the times."

Our century is one of almost incredible change, and the Church has been caught up in that change. For fifty years before Vatican II changes were taking place in the Church quietly, yet they were significant and extensive enough to lay the groundwork for the emergence of the Second Vatican Council. Some of those changes, particularly in liturgy, can be traced back to the 19th century, as will be seen later.

Le Concile De Vatican II, a recent book by Father Yves Congar, an expert on Conciliar matters, throws some interesting and new light on the beginnings of that great Council. Father Congar refers to an entry of Pope John's diary dated January 19, 1959, that indicates that the Pope got the idea of a Council that would follow his experience with the Roman Synod of 1960 and the beginning of the revision of the Code of Canon Law. He had also told his Secretary of State Cardinal Tardini of his intention to announce the idea of a Council on January 25th. On that date he would ask the clergy and faithful of Rome to be present and pray with him at the Basilica of St. Paul's Outside-The-Walls when the Roman liturgy commemorates the conversion of St. Paul and concludes the Octave of Prayer for Christian Unity.[1] He announced his plans in a private talk to 17 cardinals who had been at this ceremony. ''On that January 25th he announced his long range plan: Synod-Council-Reform of Canon Law. He would spend the rest of his pontificate making it happen.''[2]

Cardinal Tardini provided further insight on the background of the Council when on October 20, 1959, in a magistral panegyric evoking the memory of Pope Pius XII, he said that:

> It was the Pope's [Pius XII's] great conception of the papacy that led to preparation for the Ecumenical Council, to which a select group of learned ecclesiastics had been devoting themselves for years under his direction.[3]

Certainly, the idea of a Council came as a surprise to many. But to those close to Rome, especially the cardinals involved in the conclave that elected Pope John XXIII, the idea was not too unexpected. Cardinal Ruffini of Palermo, Italy, reacting to the Pope's announcement of the Council wrote on February 3, 1959:

> It was a desire that I have been fostering for twenty years, and which I expressed long ago to your predecessor, Pius XII. If it is well prepared, the Council could consider subject-matter no less copious or less important than was examined by the Council of Trent. Such an event, which has already aroused universal interest, will indeed offer a providential occasion for an invitation to the separated Churches to finally return to obedience to the Vicar of Jesus Christ.[4]

Further research I have made reveals that Monsignor Capovilla, Pope John's secretary in Venice and in Rome, confirmed the fact that the idea of a Council surfaced in the Holy Father's mind soon after his election. He denies those reports that state that the Pope ever said the idea came to him like a sudden inspiration of the Holy Spirit.

As a matter of fact, the Council was not just the result of a spontaneous decision on the part of the "impulsive" Pope John. It was made possible by the patient and assiduous work of leaders within the Church and in such fields as Scripture (Josef Geiselmann, Yves Congar, Elmer O'Brien, Marie Joseph Lagrange, Barnabas Ahern), in liturgy (Josef Jungmann, Godfrey Diekmann, Prosper Gueranger, Abbot Marmion, Louis Bouyer), and in ecumenism (Romano Guardini, Augustin Bea, Karl Adam, Gregory Baum, Vincent Hooft, the Graymoor Friars). It was the thorough, scholarly and tactful work over many years before the Council by such persons as these that created the atmosphere that really prompted Pope John to open those famous windows to let fresh air into the Church.

One "inside" story has it that many of the conservatives in the Curia were deadly afraid that the work of these biblical, liturgical and ecumenical scholars would now gain universal approval for their proposed changes through an open discussion at a Council of the Church.

Despite the critics, the Second Vatican Council was not an abrupt severance with the trend the Church had been following through most of the previous century. As I have just mentioned, the Church had been involved in changes directly or indirectly long before Pope John announced his intention to call a Council. And the Council was successful because of the fruition of seeds planted across the years, through the persistent and indefatigable efforts of those who kept in intimate touch with the life of the Church. Here are several examples.

The scriptural movement, or renewal of the way in which the Bible was to be interpreted, was a matter of study and controversy for many years. Prior to Vatican II, the Catholic Church interpreted the Bible quite literally. That is, she supported her doctrinal teachings with too little concern that the biblical writers might not have understood the culture and mores of our time. After all, they wrote in their own era. In the early part of this century, new methods of interpreting the Bible were introduced. These methods employed language analysis, literary criticism, historical facts and archaeological discoveries of ancient texts to bring new understanding to previously "taken for granted" biblical texts.

For a long time, there was a reluctance to acknowledge the use of these new methods. But then came Pope Pius XII in 1943 with his encyclical *Divino Afflante Spiritu*, which recognized the importance of these new methods of scriptural research and granted Catholic biblical scholars permission to use with prudence these new methods in interpreting the Sacred Scriptures.

Liturgy is another example of change that anticipated the decisions of Vatican II. Initially, the movement affected only the monks of Europe who were trying to improve their eucharistic liturgies by studying the historical background of the Mass. In the 1880's, liturgical reform spread beyond the monasteries to scholarly liturgists whose principal aim was to create active, intelligent and fruitful participation of the people in the liturgy of the Church. Research into the other sacraments developed the new understanding that a genuine, experiential participation in the Christian mysteries was needed, rather than a reverent or servant attention to the rituals.

The renewal of the liturgy really started in 19th century France with the Benedictine Father Prosper Gueranger who tried to make the liturgy of the Church known and loved. He was responsible for raising the standards of celebration of the liturgy and for spreading far and wide a knowledge of the beauty and theological importance of the texts used in the Church's worship. In Germany, liturgical renewal met with little success until the German bishops established a Liturgical Study Group and an Advisory Liturgical Commission that became the springboard for a number of international study meetings. Such meetings were held at Maria Laach in 1951; Lugano, Italy in 1953; Louvain, Belgium in 1954. Without doubt, the most important of these meetings was held at Assisi in Italy in 1954; it had the support of Pope Pius XII. The Pope's encyclical on the liturgy, *Mediator Dei*, just seven years earlier became the Magna Carta of the Liturgical Movement and vindicated what many felt was a fringe movement. From that, it was just a short step to Vatican II's call for renewal of the liturgy and an updating of the Church's sacramental practices.

Indeed, Vatican II's Constitution on the Sacred Liturgy, the first of that Council's documents to be approved, restored the biblical foundation of the liturgy and its didactic value, emphasized liturgy as a unifying factor and suggested the best ways to secure active and intelligent participation of the faithful. It provided a simplification of rites, the use of modern languages, and the incorporation of local or national customs and traditions. It enhanced the competence of national episcopal conferences and of individual bishops to regulate liturgical practices. The concelebration of the Mass by priests in certain circumstances was provided for. Communion under both kinds was encouraged. Thus, the renewed vision of the Church in her worship forced the abandonment of the static ecclesiology of the past 400 years since the Council of Trent.

The ecumenical movement was another factor that moved Pope John XXIII to emphasize the need for a Universal Council of the Church. Among Catholics, that movement began in France and Belgium at the turn of the century. Non-Catholics, however, were in the forefront of the movement and sought for unity not only among individual Christians but also among Churches and ecclesial communities. Pope Paul VI, in opening the second session of the Council in 1963, emphasized that question:

> What attitude will the Council adopt towards the vast number of brethren separated from us . . . what will it do? The question is quite clear. This Council itself was also called for this reason.[5]

And W. Visser 't Hooft in his report to the Central Committee of the World Council of Churches in Geneva said:

The existence of the ecumenical movement was one of the reasons for the holding of the Council.[6]

Although Catholic observers were invited to the important assemblies of the World Council of Churches in Amsterdam and Evanston, Illinois, in 1948 and in 1954, Rome forbade attendance. Later that attitude on the part of the Holy See changed. The instruction *Ecclesia Catholica* in 1950 which tended to admonish and warn, did, however, recognize the working of the Holy Spirit in the non-Catholic ecumenical movement. Dialogue opened up between Catholics and non-Catholics at least on an unofficial level.[7]

So how did Vatican II gather so much momentum? A determined Pope John XXIII would have his way. The time was ripe: devotionalism, liturgical renewal and the ecumenical movement were the fires smoldering in the Church on the eve of the Council. And there was the need for the reform of Canon Law, of priestly life and ministry and of religious life.

From his diplomatic experience Pope John looked back over the world in which he served, and wondered about the role of the Church in the world. He asked himself: "Is my Church a seed or a pearl? Is she only the pearl of great price to be preserved from all possible contamination? Or is the Church also the seed that must burrow into the world of the poor and give them new hope? Should she not penetrate the soil of the rich and the mighty that their consciences might be touched by the Gospel of Christ?" He had heard that the Church was irrelevant, that her pageantry and preoccupation with past glories obscured the message of Jesus. He worried about those people who were no longer turning to the Church for meaning; he worried about a Church too preoccupied with looking in on herself.

FOOTNOTES

(For full citations of sources, please see the Bibliography)

1. Congar, p. 45.
2. Bonnot, p. 53.
3. Congar, ibid.
4. Wenger, p. 8.
5. *Commentary*, Vol. II, p. 2, footnote.
6. Ibid.
7. AAS #42 (1950), pp. 145-147.

II.

The Bishops Come To Rome

As was indicated earlier, much of the material for this book was built on a series of lectures I gave following my four years of participation in the Second Vatican Council. Very often these lectures gave rise to many questions, and some of these involved the human side of the Council: "How did the bishops live in Rome? What kind of men were they? What was their work schedule? What did they do for recreation?"

The Invitation

The invitation to attend The Second Vatican Ecumenical Council followed on Pope John's announcement three years earlier that a Council was needed. It did not come as a surprise to most bishops. Versed in the problems of the world, they knew that the Church had to seek some form of adjustment to the changing times. Naturally, not all bishops were anxious to leave their dioceses for an indefinite stay abroad. The call to Rome specified an opening date of October 11, 1962 for the Council but not its closing date. However, once they were settled in Rome it did not take long for the bishops to get fired up with the enthusiasm generated in the first days of the meeting. Many, mired in the administrative details of their dioceses, began to enjoy the atmosphere of Rome and the

Council sessions. For some, Latin, the official language of the
Council, was a problem; and the inability to speak Italian was a
slight hindrance to enjoying life in Rome and its environs.

On February 2, 1962, like many other bishops in various parts
of the world, I received the formal invitation to be present for the
convening of the Second Vatican Council. With that invitation
there was enclosed the Apostolic Constitution *Humanae Salutis*, in
which Pope John XXIII translated into action his decision to
convene an Ecumenical Council. The Pope wrote thus to his
bishops:

> At the present time, after careful consideration and to give partici-
> pants in the council an opportunity to arrange everything in time,
> We have reached a decision to set the opening of the Second
> Vatican Ecumenical Council for the 11th day of October next. We
> have especially chosen this date because it links us with the memory
> of the great Council of Ephesus, which was of extreme importance
> in the history of the Church. We exhort, once more, all our sons,
> together with all the clergy and the Christian people to intensify
> even more their prayers to God for the happy success of this
> undertaking . . . that the fruits from this celebration may strengthen
> still more her divine energies and extend her beneficial influence in
> still greater measure to the minds of men.

Soon after the invitation came other directives relative to procedure in making living arrangements in Rome — that is, whether
bishops would arrange for and pay for their own accommodations
or whether the Vatican would need to provide room, board, and
transportation for those unable to provide for themselves. Many of
the religious orders, who had their generalates or headquarters in
Rome provided facilities, not only for the bishop-members of their
own congregations, but for other diocesan bishops and bishops
from the poorer countries of the world. Colleges and universities,
houses of study, hotels, hostels run by religious, and boarding-
houses (or pensions) gave hospitality to bishops, priests, the periti
and the observers at the Council. Very often these houses arranged

for bus transportation for the Council Fathers to and from the sessions.

On September 5, 1962, just five weeks prior to the opening of the Council, Pope John released a *motu proprio* (the technical name for a document drawn up and signed by the Pope on his own initiative) outlining in twelve chapters and twenty-five articles rules of procedure that would govern the Council sessions, the types of vesture the prelates would need for the three different types of sessions, and other housekeeping details.

Among the earliest directives was the naming of a presidential board made up of ten cardinals from nine nations. Two Americans, Francis Cardinal Spellman of New York and Albert Cardinal Meyer of Chicago, were among these chief officers. The Pope also named cardinals from the various Roman curial offices to head the ten Council commissions which in general paralleled the preparatory commissions he had set up two years earlier. About the same time, Cardinal Meyer was appointed to the Secretariat for Extraordinary Affairs to deal with any unforeseen problems.

The procedural norms included the requirement of a two-thirds majority, plus the Pope's own approval, for the enactment of any of the decrees of the Council. It was also decided by the Pope that non-Catholic observers might attend not only the public sessions but the working sessions of the Council as well. The long *motu proprio* covered all phases of Council work and spelled out not only who would be allowed to participate or aid in its work, but also provided the organizational framework in which the Council's work was to be carried out. Canon law regulated the presence of bishops and those who could be present by virtue of their special duties. There were three forms of Council sessions: the public gatherings presided over by the Pope, the general congregations or working sessions presided over by one of the ten presidents, and the sessions of the ten conciliar commissions. Later, as Vatican II moved on in its work, new rules or changes in the Pope's original *motu proprio* were introduced.

For instance, the rule of secrecy was lifted during the second session of the Council in 1963 in regard to discussions that took place on the Council floor. This was a great boon to the press corps that covered the Council proceedings. In addition, two experienced priest journalists from the Vatican Radio were commissioned to make official summaries of Council proceedings as they progressed. Although the media were not allowed into the working sessions, they were invited to daily press conferences as soon as a particular session of the Council ended.

And so it was that we were in Rome. The vast elliptical colonnades of Bernini seemed to stretch out their arms with a special welcome for the bishops who came from all over the world. More and more bishops poured into St. Peter's Square singly and in twos and threes that first morning of the Council, enjoying the bright and benign October sun. Soon, after picture-taking and conversation, they would enter into the cavernous interior of St. Peter's to begin the strenuous work lying ahead of them. Everywhere the Swiss Guards were in evidence and it became a bit unnerving to be saluted with such military heel-clicking every time you went by one of them.

The first days of the conciliar proceedings proved to be a liberal education for the bishops who were unfamiliar with Rome and the Vatican. Even many American bishops who were graduates of Roman universities and colleges, and familiar with ''romanita'' or the Italian or Roman way of doing things—were surprised with the way in which Vatican curial officials had prearranged the agenda for those first sessions of the Council. As was demonstrated in the very first meeting of the world's bishops, a ''democratic'' process took over when a score of bishops objected strongly to a prefabricated curial listing of appointees to key commissions and committees. That first session ended early so that the various national conferences of bishops might caucus and put forward their candidates for the proposed positions.

Another clash occurred about halfway through the first session when the draft document on the sources of Divine Revelation was presented for a first reading. Chapter VI goes into some detail about the disagreements that surfaced when this document was given to the Council Fathers.

So while grave problems of the Church Universal were being examined under certain rules and procedures, there was at Vatican II a side-play of the human and the humorous for the bishops, their roughly 300 periti, some 63 non-Catholic observers and 11 laypersons.

Serving the more practical needs of the bishops, collecting the votes and distributing documents, etc., were a variety of seminarians selected because of their ability to speak various languages.

The general meetings of the Council began at 9 A.M. sharp every morning with the celebration of Mass in a different rite every day. The ancient languages and chants of other cultures were an education in the fact that all is not Latin, European or Western in the Catholic Church. I remember one morning when we turned our heads toward the entrance to St. Peter's to hear the beating of tom-toms and the clashing of cymbals for an Ethiopian Rite Mass. We turned toward each other, a bishop from England, another from the United States, one from Japan, another from Holland, and raised our eyes and hands in wonderment, little realizing what we would do later in the Constitution on the Liturgy to perpetuate similar celebrations with all kinds of instruments. One of the remarks passed along the tiers of seats, attributed to a bishop from Brazil, was "What are they doing? Getting ready to boil a cardinal from the Curia?"

After the Mass ended, the ceremony of the gospels took place. A bishop, chosen each day from a different part of the world, flanked by two candle-bearers, carried the book the full length of the Council hall to a place just beside the table of the presiding prelate for the day. Most often it would be 10 or 10:30 before we actually got to work with the day's agenda. The Executive Secretary, the jovial and rotund Archbishop Pericle Felici, first made ''housekeeping'' announcements in flawless Latin. Those of us familiar with the scholastic Latin of our seminary days took delight in learning from him new phrases for directions to the men's room, the location of the coffee ''bars'' and warnings that we were not to tarry in them too long. He advised us of the day's agenda, announced the names of some twenty to thirty Council Fathers who had asked to speak, and in most friendly but firm language cautioned them that they were not to abuse the privilege and show their respect by limiting themselves to the allotted ten minutes. Now and then we had the impression that Archbishop Felici was treating us like students from his classroom, but when he did, it was always with a bit of humor.

By 11 or 11:30, many of the Fathers, who by this time had had a long morning (having risen early to get to St. Peter's), began to move into the side aisles of the nave behind the tier of seats, and go to the coffee bars hidden away in the cavernous sections of the basilica. Others stood in clusters obviously discussing an agenda item, or perhaps deciding what to do in their leisure time, or mapping out strategy to rebut something they did not like that day.

But always there were the loudspeakers that kept us informed of what was going on in the center nave of St. Peter's. It was not unusual for Archbishop Felici to interrupt our break with the announcement: ''Now that you are refreshed, come back to your seats. We will have a ballot.'' Sometimes too if the announcement contained the name of a speaker we wanted to hear, there was a rush to our seats or we politely stood along the aisles and listened. Cardinal Meyer of Chicago, Cardinal Suenens of Malines-Brussels and Bishop Emile De Smedt of Bruges were among those prelates. The latter was often responsible for presenting the ''relatio'' or summary of a document before it was to be debated. There were moments then, after heated debate, when a hush pervaded the great basilica and all ears were riveted on one man's voice.

There was absolute freedom of speech, with limits to time (usually ten minutes), and that time had to be devoted to the subject at hand. If either of these limits was exceeded the presiding Cardinal-President rang a bell, much like a sanctuary bell, that he leveled at the throat of a microphone. Or, he might say: "Venerable Father, your time is up" or, "What you say, Father, is not pertinent to the work at hand."

For purposes of convenience and identification, each Father of the Council was assigned a numbered seat which he occupied during that year's session. Since we were seated in groups of six according to the order of our appointment to the hierarchy, our seat numbers changed each year because of the deaths of a number of bishops, new appointments to the hiearchy or absence because of health, etc. Each group of seats was separated by an aisle, and in between the aisles were microphones for the convenience of those who wished to speak. Others who addressed the Council more formally or at some length spoke from a pulpit erected to the left of the Pope's throne. Six Americans were among the specially selected and trained stenographers — seminarians and priests doing graduate studies in Rome — who worked in relays taking down every word that was said. They were, as an insurance, backed up by tape recorders.

And so it was that, in Christopher Butler's words,

the prelates who marched in procession into St. Peter's that autumn day in 1962 represented a society which, for all its acceptance of the aeroplane, television and internal communications systems, was still, it might be said, living on what survived of the great medieval synthesis. It was a society of status rather than of dynamic change, of fixed formulae rather than of flexible growing insights. It was above all, and knew that it must remain, a witness to the reality of the absolute — and to the absolute significance of a group of events enacted nearly two thousand years ago in Palestine. It had a built-in tendency, in other words, towards conservatism. And it was a society which, though it made a universal claim, had come almost to the point of identifying itself with a west European tradition; this it was absent-mindedly seeking to impose both on the tiny groups

of [Eastern] Christians in communion with the See of Rome and on
the new Asian and African churches growing up from the great, but
far from sufficient, missionary efforts of the past hundred years and
facing, today, the new situation produced by political
independence.[1]

How true that was! But it is also true that the Council Fathers of
Vatican II surprised even themselves when they restudied the
products of their work over the four years of the Council, and
realized how far they had swung from the conservatism with which
they were labeled.

It should be noted also that most of the bishops who participated
in the Second Vatican Council were nominated to their specific
positions in the hierarchy via the Vatican curial network and could
be expected to reflect the conservatism that was inherent in the
curial offices in Rome. And yet, it must be concluded that the
bishops who came to Rome in 1962 realized that ''if the Church
refused to understand the world and make herself understood by it,
the world would pass her by and seek settlement of its problems
without reference to the Church's message.''[2]

Living in Rome

Loaded down with luggage because of the extra sets of vest-
ments needed for the various types of Council sessions, the 2540
bishops who attended the opening of the Second Vatican Council
soon adjusted to living in Rome. For many bishops who were
educated in Rome, the Council was an extension of their earlier
experience as students in the Eternal City. For other bishops —
who were obliged to make the periodic ''ad limina'' visits or
reports to Rome every five years on the state of their dioceses — the
Council became an extension of their obligation to keep in touch
with the Holy See that governed their lives as bishops. Others, like
myself, who were in touch with the Vatican during the years of the

Second World War, marveled at the new and traffic-plagued city on the Tiber.

The war years brought me to Rome frequently in the interest of supplying the Holy See with information and, sometimes, seeking direction for the War Relief and Refugee efforts of the United States Bishops' Conference, now known as Catholic Relief Services. Rome and Italy were familiar territory to me, and the language was no barrier. A heavy bean soup was typical fare in 1945 and 1946, but now seventeen years later as a bishop of Vatican II, I was able to enjoy "bella Roma" and its great hospitality and varied cuisine. It is probable that many of the Council Fathers put on weight with the normal menu of pasta, wine, veal and the like. It was not unusual to see a cardinal in a black cassock, other bishops, or American bishops in civilian dress (even before the Vatican ruled that the cassock was no longer "de rigueur"), eating fettucini at Alfredo's or "bollito a la Milanese" at Caesarina's near the Via Veneto. And it was not too long before bishops discovered ethnic restaurants that reminded them of home. Americans looking for hamburgers or bacon and eggs sunny-side-up discovered the Cavalieri Hilton Hotel on the Janiculum Hill overlooking the city of Rome.

However, eating out was expensive, but indulged in now and then to get away from the inevitable strain of the Council. Most often we stayed home to eat. After all, the day was long, there was that homework, or soon after dinner a meeting at the American College to discuss new positions vis-a-vis conciliar documents or mapping out strategy and selecting a spokesman for the American Conference of Bishops for the next session of the Council.

Some of us lived very well. Others struggled, especially bishops from the Third World or those from behind the Iron Curtain who were limited in the amount of money they were able to take out of their countries. Some of my Council confreres from Poland were happy to be invited out by me, and from my war years there were acquaintances still looking for help to make things easier during their stay in Rome. For me, it was another extension of my previous charitable efforts to see that old friends from the Middle East, India, and Africa tasted something of the new Rome after the war.

Our own Chicago House of Studies on the Via Sardegna where I lived the years of the Council with Cardinal Meyer, his affable secretary Monsignor Clifford Bergin, and Bishop Cletus O'Donnell, with whom I was consecrated a bishop, was superbly staffed. We lacked nothing, even including the noisy Vespas or miniature Italian motorcycles that went by our windows with red-hot mufflers throughout the night. Morning after morning, after meditation, our Mass and a hurried breakfast, we took off for St. Peter's in a rented car driven by Msgr. Bergin. Often during that short trip His Eminence would open his briefcase, pull out a sheet of paper and test on us that morning's intervention he intended to give. Most often we knew that the Cardinal would be one of the day's speakers because the evening before he had had his periti over for dinner. For us those evenings were a liberal education on some section of a conciliar document, as we listened to the conversation between Passionist Father Barnabas Mary Ahern, Jesuit Father Francis McCool and the Cardinal.

Sometimes Cardinal Meyer would suggest that Bishop O'Donnell and myself remain home for dinner to help entertain one or two of his confreres from the Presidency of the Council. Cardinal Doepfner of Germany was a frequent guest, as was Cardinal Alfrink of the Netherlands. Cardinal Tisserant was always an interesting dinner companion, since he had broad knowledge of the United States. All the American cardinals were sometime guests, especially on feast days or when there was need to remember Cardinal Meyer's birthday.

But most often it was just those of us who lived in the house. Besides Cardinal Meyer, Bishop O'Donnell, myself and Msgr. Bergin, there was the rector, Msgr. Joseph Howard, and several priest-students who changed during the four years of the Council sessions. Msgr. Paul Marcinkus, a Vatican employee and priest from the Archdiocese of Chicago, was the quasi-majordomo and was always generous in letting us use his membership at the Aqua Sancta Golf Club outside Rome.

Perhaps among the more unusual evenings for Bishop O'Donnell and myself were the frequent post-dinner soirees at a pension on the Piazza Hungaria. Here a number of American bishops lived, as well as a number of the outstanding periti that served the Council. The French Sisters who served the pension were always most gracious and helpful when on those free evenings we gathered to discuss the Council and much of the behind-the-scenes work of the commissions on which the periti served. Bishop Ernest Primeau, a seminary classmate and Ordinary of the Diocese of Manchester in New Hampshire, generally presided at these informal gatherings which became a learning opportunity for all of us.

Among the periti theologians that lived at the pension or were very-often-sought-after guests were: Father John Courtney Murray (who became famous at the Council for his defense of the Declaration on Religious Freedom); Father George Higgins (who served on the American Bishops' Press Panel); the French Dominican, Father Yves Congar; Father Hans Küng; Father Gregory Baum; the Benedictine Father Godfrey Diekmann; scripture scholar Father Eugene Maly; Monsignor Luigi Ligutti (known in the United States for his rural life apostolate and stationed in Rome at the United Nations Food and Agriculture headquarters) and very many others.

We generally dialogued late into the night. Sometimes, the next day, Cardinal Meyer, as we were returning home from a session of the Council would remark: "Hope you men had no difficulty staying awake during this morning's session." We admitted some difficulty, but always insisted on how much we learned at the 19th hole.

At one point curiosity got to His Eminence and without too much prompting he joined us on one or two evenings. Perhaps the

happiest encounter he had with our nocturnal group was the celebration of his birthday with a surprise party the Sisters at the
pension arranged for us.

Now and then American and other generalates of the many
religious orders that had their headquarters in Rome invited their
bishops over for dinner. We always welcomed the change from
Roman cuisine. On one such occasion the Felician Sisters, many of
whom were Americans stationed in Rome, invited the bishops
from Poland (some thirty of them), and the bishops of Polish
heritage from the United States, to a typical American Thanksgiv-
ing dinner.

Bishop Joseph Green of Reno/Las Vegas became a kind of
unofficial tour guide and travel agent. When he foresaw several
days, or especially a week, of non-Council activity he would poll
his brother bishops about trips to Sardinia, Sicily or Taormina and
its lovely resorts on the Mediterranean seacoast. Venice, Florence
and even the Holy Land were visited by some who brought some
vacation money with them. Some of us (and I was one of those who
wanted to learn more of Italian living) simply boarded a bus in the
center of Rome and rode to the end of the line, where we stopped
for a leisurely lunch and got back to Rome and home in time for
dinner and more Council homework.

Overall, it must be said that the world's bishops learned much
about Rome and its people, its cuisine, its fall weather and the
warmth with which shopkeepers enjoyed the presence of these
episcopal souvenir hunters. Many of us gained weight, what with
pasta at every meal and the sedentary nature of all those Council
sessions.

FOOTNOTES

(For full citations of sources, please see the Bibliography)

1. Butler, p. 9.
2. Ibid, p. 33.

III.

The Role Of The Theologians

The Second Vatican Council brought to the forefront a number of theologians, who for years prior to the Council suffered for their convictions in areas of theological speculation, yet became in large measure the authors of the theology of Vatican II.

It is important to note that the background for this apparent dichotomy can be traced to the embattled atmosphere of the last years of Pope Pius XII's reign, when his encyclical *Humani Generis* and some of its restrictive measures were adopted by the Holy Office and applied to the teachings of those pre-conciliar theologians. The encyclical itself was really meant to meet the thrust of, not to stop, the theological revival after World War II. Its ultimate prudential nature is evident in its refusal to name or censure specific persons or even titles of their works, and in its evident awareness of and interest in modern thought.

As is noted later, Pope John XXIII called many of these same theologians to Rome to help in the preparatory work of the Council. He tried to introduce a bit of balance to what were the old theological positions of many of the bishops who came to the Council. Nevertheless, old battles over the ''new theology'' cropped up again and again in the aula of St. Peter's. As one might gather from other sections of this book, the battle raged over biblical, liturgical and ecclesial renewal, openness to the modern world and ecumenism.

Anyone interested in further study of this area of the pre-conciliar and conciliar history of the state of theology in the Church might read Father George Tavard's *The Pilgrim Church*. Father Tavard shows that the Preparatory Theological Commission, as organized under Pope John XXIII by Cardinal Ottaviani, reflected the integralist point of view as was evident in many of the Cardinal's speeches. The Cardinal often emphasized his conservatism in method and his predilection for a speculative rather than a histori-cal or biblical approach to theology. His intent was always, of course, to stress the transcendental aspects of the Catholic faith over all human attitudes. If one were to make a judgment of the Commission based on the nature of the documents it issued, its purpose according to Father Tavard, and from my experience of the Council,

> was not only to assert the rights of the Church and to man and equip the fortress of faith, but also to crush all other points of view hitherto accepted in the many mansions of the Catholic Church.[1]

It appeared to me, during those early sessions of the Council in 1962, that the verbal clashes over the "new theology," over liturgical reform and over the question of Scripture and Tradition, reflected not only the disappointment of the bishops in the position of the Preparatory Theological Commission, but that Commis-sion's disregard of the majority opinion of the bishops who favored the new approach, and the renewal and reform that the Pope was asking for.

There need be no shame in admitting that many, if not most, of the bishops participating in the Council — whether speaking up, or keeping silent and taking counsel within themselves —were plunged for the first time since their seminary days into a veritable vortex of new theological speculation. They were confronted with questions that in their dioceses might have been on the periphery of their immediate interests. The bishop whose concerns had been the government of his diocese, the planning for schools, the building of churches, the intensification of the spiritual life of his people or the extension of the Kingdom of God in his diocese, now was called upon to become intensely involved in matters of the highest dogmatic importance.

The bishops of Vatican II were not, for the most part, professional or technical theologians. Most were called to the episcopacy from the ranks of the working clergy, and some, of course, were endowed with special education or training in various fields. Even so, I was convinced that the Holy Spirit was truly present in the Council given the evidence of the mounting perfection of the acts of that august gathering.

Theological leadership, prior to the Council, was mainly centered in France and Germany. This is apparent as one studies the names of the scholars who had a prominent role in the preparatory stages of Vatican II. Evident also was the scholarship of the many bishops from those same countries who were most often on their feet during the deliberations of the Council.

During the early preparation of the Council, those theologians (mainly French, with some Germans) whose activities had been restricted by Pope Pius XII, were still under a cloud. Pope John quietly lifted the ban affecting some of the most influential ones. Yet a number remained suspect to the officials of the Holy Office. While Karl Rahner and, to a lesser extent, Hans Küng had their influence, less well-known names from Germany were actually more important in the workings of the Commissions. Much of the real work was done by those in a position to mediate between the advanced French and German thinkers and the slow-moving curial theologians used to more antiquated forms of thought. According to Father Tavard, several Belgians became masters at this difficult art: G. Philips, Charles Moehler and Gustav Thils, all from the University of Louvain. [2]

More than 800 scholars, from 70 different countries and all five continents, were called to Rome by Pope John XXIII to serve on the 15 preparatory committees of the Council. Understandably, European theologians outnumbered the others. They constituted 71% of the membership. North and South America were least represented. There were 150 Italian and 74 French theologians. Despite the number of these scholars asked to assist in preparing for the Second Vatican Council, it did not take long for this large group to begin work. They served on the various pre-conciliar committees approved by Pope John and generally headed by a cardinal-member of the Roman Curia. These leading scholars, canonists, sociologists and missiologists were largely responsible for the agendas mailed to the bishops prior to the opening of the Council and the reworking of those agendas during the Council.

Among those many scholars was Monsignor Jan Willebrands, who later became a cardinal and the head of the important Secretariat for Christian Unity. A compatriot of his from Holland, the Rev. Sebastian Tromp, an eminent specialist in the theology of the Church, became the secretary of the important Theological Commission which was headed by Cardinal Ottaviani. Father Tromp is reputed to have written Pope Pius XII's encyclical *Mystici Corporis Christi* (1943). There is no doubt that Father Tromp had a hand in the preparation of many of the dogmatic drafts prepared for us bishops before we got to Rome. It was said of him that he never "lost his cool" even though much of his work was ignored by the Council Fathers.

Another scholar was the Yugoslav Franciscan Karl Balic, a noted Mariologist. Father Balic, backed by his friend Cardinal Ottaviani, tried valiantly to obtain a separate conciliar decree on the Blessed Virgin Mary. When the Council very wisely adopted the Dogmatic Constitution on the Church and decided to emphasize the role of the whole "People of God" in the economy of salvation, the treatment of the Blessed Virgin's role in this became the final chapter in that document.

Jesuit Father Henri de Lubac was another scholar who, like

Willebrands, later became a cardinal. He had been accused of being a protagonist of the "new theology" prior to the Council, and actually lost his professorship at the University of Lyons. Pope John appointed him a member of the Preparatory Theological Commission in 1961, and his influence grew during the Council when the complexion of that original Commission changed. This was especially the case when he became indispensable to Cardinal Koenig's secretariat on dialogue with non-believers. Father de Lubac had written many well-known books, the most famous being *Catholicism* and *The Drama of Atheist Humanism*.

Another Jesuit, Father Karl Rahner, was one of the foremost advisors to the German bishops at the Council. He died in 1984, and was the author of the famous twenty-volume series titled *Theological Investigations*. Like other pre-conciliar theologians he too was "muzzled" for awhile, but Pope John appointed him to the preparatory committee on the sacraments. It is known that the committee never consulted Father Rahner.

Father Rahner came to prominence very early in the first session of the Council when he authored the now famous "counter schema," the "Revelation of God and Man in Jesus Christ." This document was circulated unofficially through the Council hall as a possible alternative and mediating force during the heated debates on the two sources of Revelation. Despite support from the bishops' conferences of Austria, Belgium, France and Holland, Father Rahner's proposal never reached the light of day. The unfortunate vote of November 20, 1962, on whether to conclude discussion of the schema once and for all, forced Pope John to intervene in this debate and set up a mixed commission of theological and biblical scholars. This vote also committed Father Rahner's schema to limbo.

However, other teachings of Father Rahner's did influence the Council. His treatment of the new image of the Church — a "World Church," as he called it — found its way into the Dogmatic Constitution on the Church. His ideas on collegiality and the relationship between the Pope and the bishops, on which he wrote extensively in volume 10 of *Theological Investigations*, found their way into the Decree on the Bishops' Pastoral Office in the Church.

And then again, writing on the Second Vatican Council's challenge to theology, Father Rahner stated that it would be a mistake to represent the conciliar decrees as being of only "pastoral relevance." This would relegate them to a particular and circumscribed area, so that practically everything else would remain the same as before.

How prophetic was Father Rahner when he insisted that there can be no doubt that the Second Vatican Council created a challenge to Catholic theology! It provided theologians with a new and responsible task to interpret the Council's documents and decrees correctly within the wider scope of the free movement generated by the Council itself. As was demonstrated time and again within that movement, the planned-for decrees of some Roman theologians never came to fruition, and the fears of some about the direction the Council would take never came to pass.

The bishops in council brought change to the "neo-scholastic provenance" of the theology of the last 100 years; and for that reason the Second Vatican Council, in the positive teaching of its decrees, has in itself great theological significance. The Council was, as is so well known, very careful and circumspect in all its doctrinal statements. It scrupulously avoided making any new definitions, yet it had much to say about things that theology in the recent past had been silent on.

Among the quiet, less known theologians was the Dominican Father Marie Dominique Chenu of France, who tutored other periti of the Council such as Congar, Feret and Schillebeeckx. A very personal book on theology which he wrote but never published, and which was put on the Index, quietly circulated among ecclesiastical leadership in Europe and penetrated Council discussions. Father Chenu is not always listed among the prominent periti of Vatican

II, but was, like many others, one of those experts "the bishop brought along." Through his talks to various bishops' conferences and the help he gave bishops in preparing their interventions, Father Chenu earned for himself an influential position in the formulation of the Pastoral Constitution on the Church in the Modern World.

The most prominent of the American theologians, Jesuit Father John Courtney Murray, "a come-lately," was brought to the Council by Cardinal Spellman of New York in 1964. The so-called "American Document of Vatican II," which later became the conciliar Declaration on Religious Freedom, was the work of Father Murray. The two earlier versions of that schema, discussed in his absence, were rejected by the Secretariat for Christian Unity. It was generally known in Rome (and I had many opportunities to listen to Father Murray at our nightly get-togethers in the pension on the Piazza Hungaria) that the more the Secretariat for Christian Unity persisted in its unhistorical presentation of the problem of religious liberty as part of its schema on Ecumenism, the more decisive became Father Murray's influence among the bishops. His lectures to the American Bishops' Conference at the North American College were a turning point. He not only saved the Declaration, but with the help of the American participants in Vatican II, he succeeded in making it a distinct document of the Council.

Father Yves Congar, a French Dominican scholar, was and continues to be one of the most widely read of the conciliar theologians. His most recent work, *Le Concile De Vatican II*, a history of the Council, available at present only in French, is a veritable goldmine of information. His chapter on the role of theologians at the Council is a more insightful contribution than I have been able to provide in this account of my own experiences. Congar speaks of the beginnings of the Council and gives credence to the fact that the idea of a Council was already in the mind of Pope

Pius XII and that his successor, Pope John XXIII, was reminded of this right after the conclave that elected him Pope.

Father Congar's historical studies on the reform of the Church, the role of the laity, on separated Christians and on Jews, cast him in the role of a prophet as to what might happen at the Council. Even though Pope John appointed him to the Preparatory Commission on Theology, he was virtually ignored in curial circles. Too many higher officials in Rome remembered that, as one of the dominant figures in French theology, he was removed from teaching, prohibited from publishing and spent some years in exile at various Dominican houses in Jerusalem, Rome and even Cambridge in England. He forgave and he forgot; so enthusiastic was his support, for instance, of Vatican II's Constitution on the Sacred Liturgy, that when he tried to explain the document to a Paris audience he was pelted with eggs.

Long before the Council began in 1962, the Canadian Augustinian, Father Gregory Baum, was an early advisor to the Secretariat on Christian Unity in his special field of Jewish history. He is best known for his well-read book, *The Jews and the Gospel*, which he dedicated to his mother, who died in the Berlin holocaust of 1943.

This special listing of Vatican II periti would not be complete without the name of the brilliant Dutch Dominican theologian, Father Edward Schillebeeckx. Many of us bishops remember him for his lectures on theological issues during the many evenings we were free and able to hear him at the l'Anima, the Dutch house for higher studies in Rome. He was especially helpful when there was conciliar discussion about the idea of a special document on the Eucharist soon after Pope John had issued a text which was criticized by the Dutch hierarchy. There is also some credence to the story that Father Schillebeeckx had some influence on the thinking of Cardinal Suenens of Belgium, who introduced the idea of Schema 13, which later became the Pastoral Constitution on the Church in the Modern World.

One would have to add to the above names, those of other

scholars. Monsignor Pietro Pavan was often credited with being the writer of Pope John's encyclical *Mater et Magistra*. The German Redemptorist, Father Bernard Haring, like Father Schillebeeckx, played an important role in the fashioning of Schema 13. And there were others like Luigi Ciappi, O.P., an expert on the Magisterium of the Church; Alverno Huergo, another Dominican priest who specialized in the role of the bishop in his diocese; and finally, a present member of the Holy Office (really the new Office for the Doctrine of the Faith), another Dominican, Archbishop Jerome Hamer, who provided expert direction on the religious in the apostolate of the Church.

I have mentioned several times that Pope Pius XII's encyclical *Humani Generis* had, in some instances, a devastating effect on the work of a number of pre-conciliar theologians. Yet in fairness to the Pope, one must say that this quiet, well-read and scholarly man did much to prepare the way for the role the so-called new theology would play in the Second Vatican Council. Another of Pope Pius' encyclicals, *Divino Afflante Spiritu*, really paved the way for the biblical scholars whose influence on the Council was great.

During the Council there was praise for the periti brought to Rome by their bishops and for those who had previously been criticized. Pope Paul VI praised them at a public meeting of the Council when the Decree on the Apostolate of the Laity and the Dogmatic Constitution on Divine Revelation were promulgated:

> The second stage followed, that of the actual development of the council, and was characterized by confrontation with problems. Such a stage was a necessary accompaniment of the work of the council, which as you are well aware, was truly immense, to the special credit of the commissions and subcommissions. In these the work of the council "periti" (experts), and of certain ones in particular, was most exacting and profoundly wise. To accord them some public recognition, it was our wish that some of their number should be associated with us today in the celebration of the Divine Sacrifice.[3]

There were other occasions for praise of the periti who had given so much of themselves before, during and after the Council. Criticism, however, persisted. One eminent prelate, Archbishop John C. Heenan of Westminster, England, had these harsh words:

> The Church of God has suffered a great deal from the writings and speeches of some of the periti. These few specialists care nothing for the ordinary teaching authority of bishops—nor, I regret to say, for that of the pope. [4]

Another prelate, a bishop from the United States, rebutted the imprudence of such criticism and said that:

> He could not fail to say a word in tribute to the scholarly humility and forbearance with which the overwhelming majority of periti work.

The heart of the difficulty we bishops were experiencing that involved the theological experts at the Council was best explained by the then Abbot Christopher Butler, now the Auxiliary Bishop of Westminster:

> The new theology sought to go back behind scholastic systematizations and to find a richer inspiration in patristic theology and a foundation in biblical scholarship and theology. [5]

There were in fact two sides to Catholicism in 1962 when the Council began. The Roman Curia gave little evidence of realizing the need for far-reaching changes, as I have indicated earlier. The Church as a whole, and particularly in Western Europe, had for some time been experiencing a second spring. One early sign of this was the liturgical movement, which influenced the draft of the Constitution on the Sacred Liturgy so much that it was one of the best documents presented to the Council.

The document *Superno Dei Nutu*, through which Pope John called the bishops to Rome, set in motion what was termed by many "laboratories of theological research." The Pope himself emphasized that never had there been assembled in conciliar history,

> on so vast a scale, or in so precise and fundamental a fashion, the number of theological experts as in the case of the Second Vatican Council and who were the preliminary team that fashioned the early pages of the documents of that great Council.

In reality, the hundreds of periti the Pope called to Rome and those who accompanied their bishops to the Council, covered the whole field of problems which faced the Church in the 1960's both in regard to her inner life and her relationship to the world. The list of problems that preoccupied the Church then was staggering. Little did we bishops realize the amount of work that would be brought to our attention once the Council sessions began in October, 1962. Although the climate of the early sessions was in great measure fashioned by those many experts Pope John spoke about, it did not take long for the Council Fathers, once they got to work, to add their own knowledge and solutions to the problems facing the Church.

As is evident from other parts of this book, all was not harmony and consensus. Clashes between bishops and theologians emerged, and the world's media had a field day. One of the more significant confrontations played up by the press involved a communication we received governing the work and participation of the periti in the Council. The communique was dated December 28, 1963, and was issued by the Cardinal-President of the Council's Coordinating Committee. Archbishop Pericle Felici, Executive Secretary of the Council, reiterated those restrictions several times. They went this way:

> 1. According to the work assigned them, the Reverend periti should answer with knowledge, prudence and objectivity the questions which are put to them by the Commissions or the Council Fathers.

2. They were forbidden to lobby, organize currents of opinion or ideas or to divulge or defend publicly their personal opinions on Council matters.

3. They had to abstain from criticizing the Council or the Council Fathers, nor were they to communicate to outsiders the secret business of the Commissions.

The task, therefore, facing the experts or theologians was formidable. Almost 5000 reports had been sent to Pope John XXIII following on his request in 1959, that his brother bishops share with him their thoughts about Council agenda matters. At one point, Archbishop Felici, then Secretary of the Central Preparatory Commission, is said to have remarked: "The bishops have sent in enough material to Rome to supply ten Councils with material." Today one may find all of this material in some fifteen folio-sized volumes in any good Catholic library.

After having been presented with summations of much of that material studied by the Preparatory Commissions, Pope John XXIII, in his encyclical *Ad Petri Cathedram* of July 3, 1959, set forth with great precision the hierarchy of the problems to be faced and the ends to be accomplished by the Second Vatican Council:

> 61. This fond hope compelled Us to make public Our intention to hold an Ecumenical Council. Bishops from every part of the world will gather there to discuss serious religious topics. They will consider, in particular, the growth of the Catholic faith, the restoration of sound morals among the Christian flock, and appropriate adaptation of Church discipline to the needs and conditions of our times.
>
> 62. This event will be a wonderful spectacle of truth, unity, and charity. For those who behold it but are not one

with this Apostolic See, We hope that it will be a gentle invitation to see and find that unity for which Jesus Christ prayed so ardently to His Father in heaven.[6]

In the summer of 1962, the Holy See sent us bishops the first schemata we were to tackle that October. These included material on the sources of the Faith, the preservation of the Faith, morality, chastity, marriage, family, virginity, the mass media, and Christian unity.

I should mention that except for the subject of Christian unity, none of those proposed schemata became crucial in the early stages of our meetings. As is known, Sacred Scripture and the Liturgy involved our first interest. Altogether, there were 72 schemata prepared by the ten commissions chosen by Pope John; only a few saw the light of day in the conciliar aula of St. Peter's.

Overall, it would be a mistake to conclude that all the work the theologians put into the preparatory phases of the Council was ignored and that the Council Fathers and the theologians were in a constant state of confrontation.

Above and beyond the broadening and deepening of the scope of theology, the Council's whole attitude displayed a spirit of freedom. The desire, as Pope Paul VI put it,

> was to study first and then to make a decision, to have an awareness of problems and respect for the specialists (yet without timidly allowing them to have the last word in their professional capacity).[7]

Thus, for instance, though the Council stressed that the task of authoritatively interpreting the word of God, whether written or handed on, belongs exclusively to the Church's teaching authority, it also affirmed that the Holy Spirit effects

> a growth in understanding of the realities and the words which have
> been handed down. This happens through the contemplation and
> study made by believers . . . from the intimate understanding of
> spiritual things they experience, and through the preaching of those
> who have received through episcopal succession the sure gift of
> truth. (Dogmatic Constitution on Divine Revelation, #8).

Here, as elsewhere in the documents, cooperation between all
believers, theologians, and bishops was seen as essential. The
Council did not repeat Pius XII's view of the magisterium as the
proximate rule of faith. It stressed that the bishops who serve the
word of God must also heed those in whom the Holy Spirit has
produced special graces, experience and understanding of the
faith, although it remains the bishop's role to judge and to make use
of that understanding.

Thus, paragraph twelve of the Dogmatic Constitution on the
Church emphasizes the role of the "faith and charity" of the whole
of the People of God who share in Christ's prophetic mission. It
relies heavily on St. Paul's First Letter to the Corinthians in which
he stresses that the Holy Spirit allots His gifts "to everyone
according as He wills" (1 Cor 12:11), and that "The manifestation
of the Spirit is given to everyone for profit" (1 Cor 12:7).

Vatican II applied that exhortation practically when it urged
that more of the laity receive adequate theological formation and
that some among them even dedicate themselves professionally to
these studies and contribute to their advancement. It urged "that all
the faithful, clerical and lay, possess a lawful freedom of inquiry
and thought, and the freedom to express their minds humbly and
courageously about those matters in which they enjoy competence" (Pastoral Constitution on the Church in the Modern
World, #62).

It was apparent to the Council Fathers, very early in their
deliberations and their consultation with theologians, that the
Council was not a time for issuing anathemas but for engaging in

dialogue. It was a time in history in which to make clear the Christian meaning of man and society. As Pope John said in his opening address to the Council:

> At the outset of the Second Vatican Council, it is evident, as always, that the truth of the Lord will remain forever. We see, in fact, as one age succeeds another, that the opinions of men follow one another and exclude each other. And often errors vanish as quickly as they arise, like fog before the sun.
>
> The Church has always opposed these errors. Frequently she has condemned them with the greatest severity. Nowadays, however, the spouse of Christ prefers to make use of the medicine of mercy rather than that of severity. She considers that she meets the needs of the present day by demonstrating the validity of her teaching rather than by condemnations. Not, certainly, that there is a lack of fallacious teaching, opinions and dangerous concepts to be guarded against and dissipated. But these are so obviously in contrast with the right norm of honesty, and have produced such lethal fruits, that by now it would seem that men of themselves are inclined to condemn them, particularly those ways of life which despise God and His law, or place excessive confidence in technical progress and a well-being based exclusively on the comforts of life. They are ever more deeply convinced of the paramount dignity of the human person and of his perfecting, as well as of the duties which that implies. Even more important, experience has taught men that violence inflicted on others, the might of arms and political domination, are of no help at all in finding a happy solution to the grave problems which afflict them. [8]

Overall, one final point should be emphasized about the conciliar proceedings. The Pope allowed and encouraged full freedom of expression. No one would deny that there were conflicting opinions. There were always areas of special concern on the part of the participants of Vatican II: concern to avoid errors, to maintain and affirm doctrine, but above all to present the Church's teachings in a less scholarly and more assimilable form.

Pope Paul VI himself reacted to press reports that gave the impression of much infighting in the Council proceedings:

> If attention is limited to these externals or if it undertakes to emphasize them, then the reality of things is altered, even falsified. For all the bishops are endeavoring to avoid giving any substance to these divisions, in order on the contrary to be guided by the objective divine truth which they profess and by the fraternal charity which animates them.
>
> Certainly, discussion in the council hall is free and varied.
>
> But if it undoubtedly bears the stamp of the various backgrounds of the bishops, it is not determined, even so, by closed minds or prejudices.[9]

FOOTNOTES

(For full citations of sources, please see the Bibliography)

1. Tavard, p. 33.
2. Ibid, pp. 34-35.
3. *Council Daybook*, Vol. 3, p. 238.
4. *Council Daybook*, Vol. 2, p. 171.
5. Butler, p. 14.
6. *The Papal Encyclicals*, Vol. 5, p. 11.
7. *Council Daybook*, Vol. 2, p. 138.
8. Rynne, pp. 268-269.
9. *Council Daybook*, Vol. 1, pp. 155-156.

IV.

Significant Speakers

No discussion of the Second Vatican Council can dispense with some reference to those Council Fathers who made a significant contribution to that extraordinary gathering of the world's bishops.

One is at a loss to make a selection of the prelates who stood out in the deliberations of Vatican II that would please everyone. Again I must emphasize that I write from my own experience and observations. There are, however, others who made choices. Here are a few: *Twelve Council Fathers*, by Father Walter Abbott, S.J.; *Vatican Council Two (The First Session)*, by Antoine Wenger, A.A.; *The Pilgrim Church*, by Father George Tavard; and *Third Session, Council Speeches of Vatican II*, by William K. Leahy.

As I go back over my recollections of Vatican II, there were many Council Fathers whom I consider to have been the outstanding thinkers and speakers there.

Statistically, His Eminence, Augustin Cardinal Bea—a saintly man, slightly stooped, of sharp eye and mind, and one of the most respected biblical scholars of our time—made 66 interventions. I have been unable to trace the number of written interventions he must have presented to the Secretariat of the Council. He was revered not only by the non-Catholic and other observers of the Council, but by the bishops and especially by the media who quickly learned not to try to manipulate his direct and agile mind.

As the head of the new Secretariat for Promoting Christian Unity, the Cardinal will go into history as the great promoter of Pope John's quest for unity. He was given the rare privilege of addressing the first session of the Council with a special summation of the work on ecumenism.

On the other hand, Cardinal Ruffini of Palermo, Italy—considered to have been one of the intellectuals among the Council Fathers—claims the record for the greatest number of interventions. I have not been able to verify this claim. Like Cardinal Frings of Cologne (Germany), Lienart of Lille (France), and Meyer of Chicago, Cardinal Ruffini was an expert in scriptural studies and had profound influence in the debate on the Dogmatic Constitution on Divine Revelation.

Leon Cardinal Suenens, Archbishop of Malines-Brussels in Belgium, who spoke 63 times, is credited with inspiring the Pastoral Constitution on the Church in the Modern World. He is also credited with giving the title *Lumen Gentium* (Light of All Nations) to the Dogmatic Constitution on the Church, beyond doubt the most important and most influential document of the Council.

Julius Cardinal Doepfner, Archbishop of Munich-Fresing, also a frequent and influential speaker, became known as the "bishop of two worlds," since his archdiocese in Germany was divided by the Iron Curtain. That title served him well, since he became a great supporter of one of Pope John XXIII's principal aims for the Council, that of bringing about Christian unity against the anti-Christian forces of the world. The Cardinal was very effective in making contact with and in encouraging the participation of the bishops from Poland in the Council.

Among the Americans, Cardinal Spellman of New York spoke most frequently. Father Vincent Yzermans in his book *American Participation in the Second Vatican Council* reports that the Cardinal made 131 oral and written interventions, speaking on every conciliar schema. His intervention on the rights of children and parents to Catholic education greatly influenced the Declaration on Christian Education.

The Archbishop of Chicago, Cardinal Meyer was beyond doubt among the most highly respected of the Council Fathers. He was one of the twelve Council presidents and an outstanding Scripture scholar. It was said of him that:

It was, nonetheless, quite generally recognized that Cardinal Meyer was a voice to be heeded. On more than one occasion members of other hierarchies approached him after his intervention to ask for copies of his address. In one commission meeting an American consultant overheard a group of French bishops remark, as they were discussing a crucial issue: ''We had better consult Meyer on this. His judgment would be most valuable.'' It is a known fact among those closely associated with the Council that both Cardinal Suenens and Cardinal Alfrink diligently made efforts to cultivate the friendship and the subtle influence of Cardinal Meyer among the Americans. [1]

Very often some of the other bishops would approach Bishop O'Donnell or myself, knowing that we lived with the Cardinal in Rome, and ask if we knew His Eminence's position on certain of the debated issues. We were, of course, privy to the conversations at the dinner table when the Cardinal invited one or another of his confreres from the College of Cardinals, or when his periti were present. Rarely, however, were we in a position to reveal confidences unless the Cardinal authorized us to do so.

Other Americans, of course, played an important role in the Council. Father Yzermans, in his *American Participation in the Second Vatican Council*, provides a comprehensive list of them.

One of my favorite Council Fathers, and probably the most popular, was Bishop Emile De Smedt of Bruges in Belgium. Bishop De Smedt was responsible for introducing several of the Vatican II documents to the Council. His summaries (*relatio*), as they were termed, were fantastic pieces of clarity and directness, and he was often applauded (against Council rules) for his presentations.

He will, however, go down in history for his famous speech on the childish attitude of triumphalism, juridicism and clericalism that was so often displayed by the Roman theologians vis-a-vis the draft of the Dogmatic Constitution on the Church.

Perhaps the strongest intervention in favor of the use of the vernacular languages in the Mass was made by Patriarch Maximos IV Saigh, who represented the ancient Church of Antioch. The Patriarch made an imposing figure in the flowing robes of the Melkite Church. Although Latin was the official language of the Council, he spoke in French to emphasize the point that Latin should not be considered the sole language of the Church. He was an effective speaker, and won his point when he emphasized that our Lord spoke the language of His contemporaries. One of the most challenging statements made by the Patriarch had to do with the appointment of bishops. He felt that these appointments did not belong to the Pope by divine right, but that bishops should be appointed by a synod of bishops, as is the practice among the Melkites.

Eugene Cardinal Tisserant, the dean of the College of Cardinals, was always a colorful presenter of his views on many of the Council documents. As head of the Vatican Library, he had access to archives and other pertinent material that brought life to his interventions. His learned presentation of the history and impact of language among various peoples had a telling effect on the Conciliar vote in favor of the use of the vernacular in the celebration of the Mass.

Another Cardinal of French background, Paul Leger of Canada, addressed the Council more than 40 times. He caused a sensation when in addition to favoring communion under both species and the use of the vernacular at Mass, he came out for the concelebration of Mass by groups of priests. The arch-conservative protector of the doctrine of the Church, Cardinal Ottaviani, is said to have reacted (as we younger bishops got the story in the rear of St. Peter's) with, "Is the Cardinal about to lead a revolution?"

But of Cardinal Ottaviani this must be said: despite his infirmities and almost total blindness in both eyes, he rose many times to speak from memory and in flawless Latin of the rich heritage of the Church he loved. His interventions were never dull, sometimes protracted (to the chagrin of the Presiding Cardinal), but substantive and above all firm. At one point, he absented himself for a week from the Council sessions because he could not have his way.

Giacomo Cardinal Lercaro of Bologna, considered a peacemaker among the Italian bishops (who often supported the position of the Roman Curia at the Council), was very closely listened to when he rose to speak. His most effective presentations were in the field of liturgy, so much so that he was rewarded with the presidency of the Council's Liturgical Commission. Early in the second session of the Council, Lercaro was instrumental in winning over the bishops to a procedural change: namely, that speakers coordinate their views with that of their episcopal conferences. The Cardinal was hinting that one or two bishops should speak for an entire conference, thus lessening the number of speakers asking to be heard. He also hinted that such representatives be given particular attention.

Cardinal Frings of Cologne, a Council president and close friend of Cardinal Meyer of Chicago, not only made a significant contribution to many of the documents of Vatican II, but with Cardinal Lienart of France was responsible for the sensational rejection of the membership on the ten new commissions that confronted the bishops on the very first day of the Council.

Suspecting that the Vatican offices had "packed" these commissions with favorable people, Cardinal Frings, together with his friend from France, had the courage to suggest that the Council adjourn until such time as the bishops had time to get to know each other and their talents. Afraid that Cardinal Lienart's French-accented Latin was not understood, the German Cardinal, an effective and powerful speaker, repeated the intervention in what later became known as the Franco-German alliance. This not only gave the Council Fathers an early day off, but gave a portent of the future relationship between the Council membership and those who would try to manipulate its agenda.

Some of my neighbors in those tiers of seats and myself got from this our first hint of what ''renewal'' was going to be about, let alone a practical demonstration of Pope John's ''aggiorna-mento''!

Cardinals seem, from this listing, to predominate. Theirs was a privileged position. They were always the first to speak as the day's session began, and so lengthy was the list of speakers, that many bishops never got their turn. But the list of bishops who dominated the Council sessions was great. After all, they outnumbered the cardinals.

At least some of those prelates like Luigi Carli of Segni, Italy; Marcos McGrath of Panama; Gabriel Garrone of Toulouse, France; Eugene D'Souza of India; Philip Hannan and Charles Helmsing of the United States ought to be mentioned. Then there were several abbots and other heads of religious orders that made outstanding contributions to the work of the Council. Among them were Abbot Christopher Butler who later became the Auxiliary Bishop of Westminster, and whom I quote often in this book because of his theological understanding of the documents of Vatican II. Father Pedro Arrupe, head of the Society of Jesus, often spoke on matters that concerned the religious.

But no list could be complete without the name of Archbishop Pericle Felici, the genial, even entertaining conservative servant of the Council. Its General Secretary, his mellifluous and vibrant Latin was most often heard throughout the expanse of St. Peter's Basilica. Frequently the Archbishop made us feel like we were in a classroom at the old seminary. He was a teacher, but more of a taskmaster; ingratiating, yet suspected of intrigue. We bishops sometimes found it hard to understand whether he was speaking for the Holy Father or interpreting the Pope "in his own words." A bishop-doodler near me loved to portray Felici in cap and gown with a ruler in one hand and an apple in the other.

FOOTNOTES

(For full citations of sources, please see the Bibliography)

1. Yzermans, p. 8.

V.

The New Image Of The Church

With the passage and promulgation on November 11, 1964, of the Dogmatic Constitution on the Church (*Lumen Gentium*) the Church as an institution and (as that document itself uses the expression) "as the People of God," would never be the same. A new and comprehensive ecclesiology was sorely needed to not only complete but build on the work started in that area by the First Vatican Council in 1869.

We might recall that it was the Reformation that challenged the Church to define her own nature, to clarify her role and to vindicate her exercise of authority in purely religious matters. In response to Protestantism, the theology of the Church tended to emphasize her hierarchical and institutional dimensions; it emphasized structure, authority, the sacred power of the Pope, bishops and clergy. There were 400 years of this theology until Vatican II launched a new definition of the Church, her nature and her mission.

This new image of the Church is succinctly expressed in the very first paragraph of the Dogmatic Constitution on the Church, where she is described as a sacrament, or a sign and instrument of "intimate union with God" and of that union which Christians have with God and with one another.

As the renowned liturgist, Benedictine Father Godfrey Diekmann, put it so well,

> The bishops of the world discovered at Vatican II the catholicity of the Church. They experienced the living, existential Church, with its staggeringly diversified problems and needs and hopes. Ecclesiology could never again be for them a schoolbook abstraction, described in neat categories. The living Church, in the person of its bishops, had, as never before in its history, become aware of itself, its nature and mission, and each succeeding week of common effort and personal contacts (during the Council) brought new disclosures. The Council itself was, in effect, the most potent catalyst for a truly contemporary ecclesiology. [1]

In the opinion of many, and in the perspective of just these few decades after the Council, the Dogmatic Constitution on the Church is *the* seminal document of the Second Vatican Council. It is the one which, during the four years of our work, exerted the most influence on the other documents we studied. Next to the impact that the Constitution on the Sacred Liturgy has had upon the daily life of the faithful, the document on the Church will have a lasting influence in that area that theologians today call *communio*, that is, the extension of "Church-mindedness" to the whole of the People of God. In other words, *communio* is what has already become a familiar practice, the sharing of responsibility for the goals and mission of the Church by everyone.

Perhaps the best summary of what the bishops were thinking about came out of remarks made by the Coadjutor Bishop of Strasbourg, Arthur Elchinger whom I must quote verbatim. This genial bishop charmed us with this analysis:

> Yesterday the Church was considered above all as an institution, today it is experienced as a community. Yesterday, it was the Pope who was mainly in view, today the Pope is thought of as united to the bishops. Yesterday the bishop alone was considered, today all the bishops together. Yesterday theology stressed the importance of

the hierarchy, today it is discovering the people of God. Yesterday it was chiefly concerned with what divided, today it voices all that unites. Yesterday the theology of the Church was mainly pre-occupied with the inward life of the Church, today it sees the Church as orientated to the outside world.[2]

This new concept of the Church of the future was not easy to come by. Toward the end of the first session of the Council, the bishops were mindful of their disappointments in the struggle over the schema on the sources of Revelation which almost precipitated the end of the Second Vatican Council, and their worsening relationship with the Theological Commission. They sensed the need for setting forth with determination a new vision of the Church, a more biblical, vital and dynamic vision.

Bishop Emile De Smedt of Bruges made the most sensational intervention during that troubled first session of the Council when he criticized not only the general tone of the draft schema of the Church, but urged that all sense of "triumphalism" be avoided in describing the mission of the Church; that "clericalism" which so fascinated the ordained give way to the place the laity also have in the mission of the Church; and that "juridicalism," which dominated the interpretation of doctrine, be replaced with a more evangelical, more gospel- and service-oriented teaching instrumentality. The general feeling of the Council Fathers was that when the Church preaches the truths of faith, she should do so with patience and kindness, without assuming a strictly juridic stance, that she show herself as a patient and merciful mother towards all.

At the end of the first session, the bishops returned home to find their flocks anxious to learn what really happened during those months they were in Rome. The media had reported stormy meetings over the meaning of the Church, the interpretation of Sacred Scripture and the portent of changes in the liturgy.

Amid delayed administrative decisions that had to be made, the bishops, in moving about their dioceses, sensed a deep responsibility; they had not only to interpret what actually happened in the discussions at the Council, but in the process, had to measure the effect the new image of the Church was having on the faithful.

Many bishops, like myself, were asked to speak to groups of clergy and laity. In preparation for such talks, they had necessarily to return to the homework they did in Rome. They soon learned that the intervals between sessions of the Council became opportunities to gain both new knowledge of the orientation of their flocks toward the Council, and for themselves a better preparation for the trip back to Rome.

Pope John XXIII must have sensed the desires of the bishops while listening to their discussions during the first session of the Council over the closed circuit television he had installed in his apartment. When they returned to Rome for the second meeting, his successor, Pope Paul VI, greeted them with the assurance that not only the schema on the Church would be revised in the light of the perspectives opened up by their interventions, but that their other common concerns for the success of the Council would be respected.

Consequently, the beginnings of the second session of the Council were without incident. Although the bishops were now faced with a completely rewritten text on the nature of the Church (and even though this new text did not reflect all of the suggestions made by the 76 bishops who spoke a year earlier on the schema), it provided some hope for working out the new image of the Church, that Pope John XXIII had called for.

The first reaction to the new schema came from Cardinal Suenens of Belgium, who disliked the order of the chapters. He succeeded in having the chapter on the People of God placed at the beginning of the document, right after consideration of the Church as Mystery. His reasoning, that the bishops, priests and laity all belonged to God's People, won the approval of the Council Fathers even though the change was not willingly accepted by the Theological Commission.

Thus it was that in chapter 2 of the Dogmatic Constitution on the Church, the laity discovered their new role in the Church by virtue of their ''common priesthood.'' Article 10 puts it this way:

> The baptized, by regeneration and the anointing of the Holy Spirit, are consecrated into a spiritual house and a holy priesthood. . . . Though they differ from one another in essence and not only in degree, the common priesthood of the faithful and the ministerial or hierarchical priesthood are nonetheless interrelated. Each of them in its own special way is a participation in the priesthood of Christ.

Article 33 in the fourth chapter of the document is even more specific:

> The lay apostolate, however, is a participation in the saving mission of the Church itself.

The title and contents of chapter 2 of the Dogmatic Constitution on the Church, as the People of God, is therefore a moving example of the basic orientation Pope John XXIII desired of Vatican II. It speaks well of the profound desire of the Council Fathers who sought to put greater emphasis on the human and communal side of the Church, rather than on the institutional and hierarchical aspects. These latter, as I indicated earlier, were stressed through all the centuries following the Council of Trent (1545-1563). Overall, the Second Vatican Council was concerned with the Church's basic understanding of herself, one that is people-oriented.

Shared responsibility is probably the keynote of the Dogmatic Constitution on the Church. The chapter on the nature of the episcopal office, its relationship to the Pope, and the sacramental nature of that office, was the most debated. We struggled over the word ''college'' out of which grew the much abused term ''collegiality.'' Can the Holy Father share the primacy of his office with the bishops? How do bishops share the power of their office with their priests and the laity whom they serve? These were burning questions to which an answer had to be found. That is, if together, as a People of God, there is sharing in direct service, in planning, in management and in the creation of new ways of carrying out the mission Christ entrusted to His Church.

Perhaps we now need to ask: What are the implications of the new instruments of shared responsibility, this emphasis on all the faithful, bishop, priest and laity being the People of God and sharing in the mission of the Church? Theologians are asking today, as we bishops asked in 1963, how there can be collegial acts other than the two mentioned in the Dogmatic Constitution on the Church: namely, the action of an Ecumenical Council and the action of the entire college of bishops dispersed throughout the world acting in union with the Pope. What is, on the other hand, the influence and power of the Synod of Bishops that meets periodically as an advisory body to the Pope? What of the influence and power of a national conference of bishops? What are the implications at the level of diocesan pastoral councils, presbyteral councils and parish councils? And, one might add, given the proliferation of organizations opposing change in the Church, is there one teaching magisterium in the Church, or another, false one born of the misunderstandings that came out of the Council?

Most of these questions were discussed during the second session of Vatican II in 1963. But doubt and concern exist to this day in what appears to be a watering down of the good intentions engendered by the bishops when they embraced the concept of shared responsibility at all levels in the Church. The models and pastoral practices of the Church in general have indeed undergone radical change. But in some instances, even in Rome, at the national level of Bishops' Conferences and in a number of dioceses, there persists an inclination toward a type of centralization of decision-making that smacks of a pre-conciliar mentality.

The whole problem in 1963, and today, revolves around an understanding of the word "college." The weightiest objection to the use of the term is that the college of bishops could endanger the primacy of the Pope.

Cardinal Suenens of Belgium, who gave the title *Lumen Gentium* to the Dogmatic Constitution on the Church, suffered much for his defense of the concept of collegiality. At one of those early fall evening meetings at the Dutch College in Rome during the Council, he told a group of us that defining the collegiality of bishops and their relationship to the Pope filled in the gaps left by the First Vatican Council when it discussed the primacy of the Roman Pontiff. He was prophetic in telling us that the consequences of collegiality for the Pope in his relationship to the bishops would cause serious problems in the future. In an interview after the first session of the Council, Cardinal Suenens said:

> I am sure that the next session of the Council will see a study of the relationship between the Pope and the bishops. I hope that the definition of papal infallibility which was made at the First Vatican Council will be re-presented in a manner that will remove many misunderstandings on the part of Protestants and members of the Orthodox churches. We must stress the collegiality of the bishops, the fact that the college of bishops is a body of bishops descended from the twelve Apostles united under the leadership of Peter and his successors. By our attention to the fact of the collegiality of the bishops, we will show the Orthodox that we are thinking along a line that means so much to them. Moreover, by stressing the role of the laity in the Church, we will reassure the Protestants that we hold something very dear to them—the sharing of the people in the royal priesthood of Christ. Thus, the Second Vatican Council will be an act of charity to our separated brethren—Orthodox, Anglicans and Protestants—just as it will be an act of charity to Catholics in its return to the purity of the Gospel message. [3]

Chapter 3 of the Dogmatic Constitution on the Church, which devotes so much space to the bishop in the hierarchical structure of the Church, is related to another document of the Council, the Decree on the Bishop's Pastoral Office in the Church. This latter document was originally a part of the schema on the Church under the title of "Bishops and Diocesan Government," as well as part of another, "On the Care of Souls." The latter was finally incorporated into the schema on Bishops and Diocesan Government in accord with the wishes of many of the Council Fathers. The commission in charge of putting the two documents together in late 1963 presented the bishops with a new draft to which they gave the title, "On the Bishops' Pastoral Office in the Church." But it was not until the Spring of 1964 that we bishops received the revised draft of that schema. In the fall of that year began what would be the final phases of the discussion that gave us the Decree on the Bishops' Pastoral Office in the Church.

The Dogmatic Constitution on the Church defined episcopal consecration as a sacrament, and defined the canonical mission of the bishop as this relates to his teaching office and his collegial position within the concept of the Church as the People of God. Except for this, it had too little to say about the pastoral role of the bishop in the Church. The Decree just mentioned, therefore, provides some interesting highlights on the bishop's role and responsibilities, some of which could not be contained within the theme of the Dogmatic Constitution.

At this point I would also point out that if too little was said in the Dogmatic Constitution on the Church about the bishop's role in the Church, the priesthood received lesser notice. A mere ten lines of text were devoted to the priesthood, and these emphasized the priest's total dependence on, and orientation toward his bishop. The only positive statements were reflected in the priest's personal relationship to Christ and the privilege he enjoyed in celebrating the Eucharist and administering the other sacraments.

What was surprising about the meager treatment of the role of the priest is that when Pope John XXIII had sent us a questionnaire seeking suggestions for an agenda for the Council, an overwhelming desire for a special document on the priesthood was manifested. The Pope recognized the need for such a singular document on the priesthood, but the commission he set up on the Discipline of Clergy and the Christian People, perhaps for lack of time or the vagueness of their mandate, produced the limited treatment that brought vehement reaction from a good number of the bishops at the Council. To allude to just a few of the interventions: Archbishop Conway of Ireland asked for a whole chapter on the priesthood in the schema on the Church. Archbishop Dennis Hurley of South Africa bemoaned the fact that the priesthood was treated so casually in the schema. The bishop, he felt, was often remote to and sometimes even an unknown figure to the people. The priest was his eyes and ears, his hands and feet, the very voice of the bishop. To handle the bishop's closest collaborator in this manner was a disgrace.

These interventions and many others had some effect. By the end of the second session in 1963, we were presented with a new schema on the priesthood called *De Sacerdotibus*. But alas, this turned out to be a document of twelve guiding principles that only caused more furor in the Council. It was manifestly juridical rather than pastoral in tone. It stressed the duties of the priest and was much too preoccupied with discipline and obligation, rather than with the fatherly and spiritual relationship that ought to exist between the bishop and his priests. Very soon, the coffee bars behind the nave of St. Peter's began to buzz with the expression: *The priest, the forgotten man of the Council.*

Then, to add more wood to the fire, Archbishop Francis Marty of Rheims, speaking for the commission on the priesthood at the third session stunned all of us with the news that, at long last (and this was October 1964) a new document was ready on the priesthood. He called it a "Proposition" that spelled out the pastoral needs of the ministry in a positive manner. After 41 critical interventions that day, Cardinal Meyer of Chicago was given the microphone. He expressed for all of us, not only our profound disappointment, but embarrassment that the Council would dare to reduce the nature and purpose of the priesthood to a set of paternalistic propositions. Needless to say, thunderous applause came after the Cardinal's words, and from that point on the so-called schema on the priesthood in its present form was doomed.

However, as was the practice in the treatment of the other documents of Vatican II, to the publicly expressed comments of the bishops were added a list of written interventions. There poured in 455 of these on the priesthood after Archbishop Marty's presentation. The responsible commission brought these together in a booklet of some 44 pages. Just before our departure for home toward the end of the third session, we were advised to study the booklet and send in our written observations prior to the next session. On October 13, 1965, almost at the end of the Council, and two years after the first schema on the priesthood was given us, we were given the final draft of a document that became the Vatican II contribution on the priesthood: the Decree on the Ministry and Life of Priests.

It probably should be noted here that with the presentation of that final draft to the bishops came a letter from Pope Paul VI stating that: ''Without impending in any way the liberty of the Fathers'' to express their opinion, it was his judgment that:

> Public debate [on priestly celibacy] is not opportune on this subject which is so important and which demands such profound prudence. Furthermore it is our intention not only to maintain this ancient, sacred and providential law with all the force of which we are capable, but also to reinforce its observance . . .''[4]

On December 7, 1965, the day before the Second Vatican Council came to a close, Pope Paul VI officially promulgated the document on the priesthood. On that day it, together with other relevant statements in other conciliar documents, became a guide for priests. I would like to stress just two of the many highpoints of the Decree on the Ministry and Life of Priests. Chapter 2 in explaining the priestly functions names the three offices, those of preaching, governing and sanctifying. It is interesting that as this threefold role of the priest's mission is developed in article 2 of the

Decree, the order in which those obligations are listed is not without significance, especially today when there is so much confusion and misunderstanding about the role of ministry and priesthood. The commission to preach comes first. It emerges out of the faith and tradition of the Church. It must put this faith into words especially at the daily celebration of the Eucharist, as the Constitution on the Sacred Liturgy advises.

As for the confusion that exists today because of a proliferation of ministries, great hope is put into the Synod of Bishops scheduled for 1987 for a theology of ministry that will make clearer the role of the ordained and non-ordained who serve the needs of the Church.

Another highpoint of the Decree stresses the life of priests and how that life relates to the continuing need for vocations. Article 12 asks for a clear distinction between the priest's ministry or office and his life or status. So many of the interventions we listened to during the final arguments for the Decree, stressed that we could attract more vocations if that special union with Christ (and hence between the priest and Christ's mission) were emphasized, rather than the idea of status. Out of my experience, the priest needs to be able to answer the interested young man's question: Do you know Christ?

Behind the scenes during the drafting of what was to become the Decree on the Bishop's Pastoral Office in the Church, there was input from the higher echelon of the religious orders, certain members of the Roman Curia, not a few bishops, and a number of Catholic universities, regarding the selection of bishops, the power of bishops at the level of the local Church, and the position of titular or auxiliary bishops.

As an auxiliary bishop I listened with keen interest to the debates that surfaced when the draft document was presented to us in the Council. After all, the auxiliary bishop (at least as I sensed my role and as other auxiliary bishops with whom I spoke envisioned theirs) was, more or less, a glorified priest with a role akin to that of a retired bishop. The auxiliary bishop had no vote in many of the episcopal conferences, his expertise or experience was not called for, and he generally was restricted to administering the sacrament of confirmation in his diocese.

To dismiss this subject briefly, I must say that the Council decided that the measure of the auxiliary bishop's powers should be determined by the tasks entrusted to him by the residential bishop. And that is the general practice today. As for the retired bishop, the language in article 21 of the final decree is even more vague.

When the discussion on the Dogmatic Constitution on the Church finally ended, many bishops felt that the thorny subject of collegiality was put to rest. Not so. Even though the principle of collegiality was approved earlier by the majority of the bishops, it had yet to be legally established. And that opened up again the proverbial "can of worms."

Again, I must allude to Cardinal Suenens' prophetic vision of the problem we would have with the concept of collegiality. As we moved into discussing the legal ramifications of shared responsibility, it became ever more clear that we would have difficulties unless a "theology of collegiality" was agreed upon. And this was the trend of thought in the minds of many of the Council Fathers when we tried to bring together practical applications of the concept not only in our dioceses, but at that higher plateau of our collaboration with the Holy Father in the government of the Church.

Because shared responsibility was, as I said earlier, at the heart of the Dogmatic Constitution on the Church, several bishops proposed that perhaps the document ought to have a new title like, "The Practice of Collegiality." But really, what bothered most of the Council Fathers was that unless a doctrine or theology was established, the concept of shared responsibility would suffer when other sensitive areas of relationships would come up. For instance, there was on future agenda the application of the principle of collegiality to a Synod of Bishops that would meet with the Pope periodically; the relation of bishops to the Roman Curia; and further down the line, the role of the National Conferences of Bishops as well as the position of the bishop in his diocese vis-a-vis his collaboration with a Presbyteral Council, a Diocesan Council of advisors, and then finally, the relation of the parish priest to his Parish Council. All of these instrumentalities that we know today, and which have come to us out of the Second Vatican Council, still do not have a clearly defined doctrine or theology.

As a result, at least in my opinion, the opponents of shared responsibility at all those levels I mentioned, are enjoying the excuse of ''I told you so,'' and are using circumvention to deny bishop, priest and layperson the Christian application of the law of love as Christ gave it to us. The Pope struggles in prayer as to how far he can extend himself to embrace the bishops in sharing with him leadership in the Church. There are bishops who have yet to realize that their responsibility to govern is best exemplified in loving service to those they were called to teach and sanctify. There are priests who have yet to learn that Pope John XXIII called for renewal in the Church, and not restoration of the unbending principles that were mistakenly applied to previous practices of Church life and discipline.

Admittedly, the new Code of Canon Law legislates the instrumentalities of shared responsibility I write about here. Since, in the words of John Paul II, that Code, ''appeared to be definitely desired and requested by the Council . . . and derives from one and the same intention, the renewal of Christian living . . . and that it corresponds perfectly with the teaching and character of the Second Vatican Council,''[5] it would be the hope of the bishops of that Council who voted for the concept of shared responsibility that this principle would be vigorously applied at all levels of the Church.

To complete, in a sense, this circle of complaint or criticism of how certain of the People of God were treated in the early considerations of the Dogmatic Constitution on the Church, the laity also were not given their rightful place in the schema. At least, unlike the treatment of the priesthood, the laity had dedicated to them a whole chapter, even though it only consisted of six pages of print, a half page of notes and almost three pages of commentary. And, when more time was allowed (toward the end of the second session in 1963) to discussion of the role of the laity in the Church, the faithful gained a new title in the schema: "On the People of God, particularly the Laity."

An interesting intervention was made by a classmate of mine, Bishop Ernest Primeau of Manchester, New Hampshire, at the time we were struggling with the role of the laity in the Church. In a somewhat facetious manner he said:

> Certainly we must avoid the danger of generalization; none-theless we can affirm that lay people today, conscious of their capabilities, will not allow themselves to be treated as in past times as merely passive members of the Church, blindly bowing to authority, or as mute sheep.
>
> On the contrary, there are many well-educated faithful who ask to be heard on questions of undertakings in which they have a competence that clerics more often than not lack.
>
> They want to share in the apostolic work of the Church and they certainly intend to do this under the direction of the hierarchy, but not without previously being heard by the hierarchy concerning matters within their competence. They expect the confidence of the hierarchy. . . .
>
> If we keep all this in mind, it seems that some parts of chapter three hinder more than help the vital apostolate of the laity; for example, especially number 26, page 10. The text is too negative, perhaps too cautious, and too clerical.
>
> The text insists too much on the need of obedience, reverence and subjection and does not sufficiently emphasize proper responsi-bility and freedom of action, as the proper possession of laity who are true members of the Mystical Body of Christ. Let this constant talk of their duty of subjection and reverence cease—as if their only duty be stated in these terms: believe, pray, pay and obey.[6]

That evening, I accompanied Bishop Primeau to the usual press conference held soon after the daily sessions of the Council ended. A mutual friend of ours and a peritus, Monsignor George Higgins, described in summary fashion the day's proceedings, this way:

> If the council does not give this stimulus to lay initiative, I see little hope of getting Catholics to help reform society. I have been in the social action field for 20 years, and I know that we bishops cannot do it . . . there is substantial agreement in the United States on how religious principles can be brought to bear on many of the problems of society. . . . What has been lacking in large part is a sufficient degree of interfaith cooperation in the social order to bring religious principles to bear on the social order. But we are moving in the right direction.[7]

But it was not until September 30, 1964, during the third session of Vatican II, that the fourth chapter of the schema on the Church, that treated of the laity, was introduced and earned the approval of most of the bishops. An American member of the Theological Commission, Bishop John Wright of Pittsburgh, introduced the chapter and assured us that our wishes were hearkened to in many respects. For instance:

> Bishop Wright said that efforts had been made to give a positive expression to the layman in conceptual and doctrinal terms. He said the text does not present a definition of the layman as much as it tries to describe him.
>
> Dealing with the role of the hierarchy and how the Church is formed, Bishop Wright said that an attempt had been made to steer a middle course and to avoid identifying the laity and the Church's ministers as one but also to avoid the chasm separating one from the other too absolutely.
>
> Lastly, a new paragraph had been inserted dealing with the layman's participation in the Church and its worship and as a witness of Christ. There is also greater stress on the dignity of the layman as being one of the people of God and note is paid to the apostolic significance of Christian marriage and family life. Other

points that were clarified were the rights and duties of laymen toward their superiors in the Church, Christian liberty and obedience, and free cooperation and loyalty to pastors.[8]

The crowning achievement of the whole Dogmatic Constitution on the Church is the inspiring chapter (#5) on the Universal Call to Holiness of the People of God. The Church, being a society, cannot possibly escape involvement in history, in the political, social, economic and cultural affairs of man. To be effective, to rely on the real source of its strength it needs to be a Church that is a work of grace, "a sign and instrument of intimate union with God." Her chief weapon needs always to be faith in the power of God dwelling within her, a self-sacrificing love for all people manifested to the world by the holiness of its members, by the proofs that they give of faith, hope and love, by the charismata whereby the Spirit keeps calling them to some special kind of service and equips them for it (cf. #39).

FOOTNOTES

(For full citations of sources, please see the Bibliography)

1. Yzermans, pp. 74-75.
2. *Commentary*, Vol. 1, p. 108.
3. Abbott, *Twelve Council Fathers*, p. 41.
4. Yzermans, p. 477.
5. *Code of Canon Law*, p. xii.
6. Yzermans, p. 68.
7. *Council Daybook*, Vol. 1, p. 108.
8. *Council Daybook*, Vol. 2, p. 84.

VI.

Word And Sacrament

Since there is such an intimate connection between the celebration of the sacraments, especially the liturgy, and the interpretation of the Sacred Scriptures, I thought it best to bring together the two documents that came out of the Second Vatican Council on these subjects. After all, both documents were the first to come to the attention of the bishops at the very beginning of the Council. Then also, I propose to follow the historical development of *Dei Verbum*, the Dogmatic Constitution on Divine Revelation, and *Sacrosanctum Concilium*, the Constitution on the Sacred Liturgy as they were presented to us in the first session.

Vatican II officially opened on October 11, 1962, but it took eleven days to set up the housekeeping details that were to govern the work of the Council: the appointment of ten Council commissions, the preparation of rules and procedures, and a message of the bishops to the peoples of the world calling for peace and social justice for all mankind. At the fourth general meeting of the Council, on October 22, 1962, the real work began with the project on the sacred liturgy.

Out of curiosity, I attended the press panel that evening. It was sponsored by the United States hierarchy and was to become an invaluable service to newsmen seeking competent and reliable sources of information about the Council's work. The important question that day was: "Why was the liturgy chosen as the first subject for discussion?"

The press office bulletin had a ready answer. Liturgy was scheduled as the first topic because the Council's primary task was to be directed toward an internal renewal of the Church. But then, as the Council developed, a greater emphasis was directed toward the external or outward thrust of the Church to the world. I might add that liturgy was not only the easiest of the subjects but the most familiar for the fledgling bishops who had come to Rome. Also, most of the bishops anticipated that the pastoral needs of the faithful back home would have a high priority. The Pope confirmed those hopes in his opening address, when he told us not to be preoccupied with doctrinal matters but to concentrate on the central problems. The celebration of the liturgy and sacraments was one of those.

Anticipation reigned high during those early days of our meetings in Rome. Shopping and dining out in the pleasant afternoons and evenings in the Eternal City were a form of relaxation and an opportunity to adjust to the way things were done in Rome. We did need to remember our families and friends back home, and souvenir hunting was not only another pastime, but very often the first subject of conversation as we settled down to work in the very narrow confines of our desks in St. Peter's.

Like most tourists, except that we bishops had the opportunity for a longer stay, we shared the addresses of the best places to buy things. Of course, the clerical haberdasheries did a land-office business. Episcopal vesture was novel, in good taste and cheaper in Rome.

But about halfway through the first session of the Council, while we were still talking and voting on changes in the liturgy, the subject of the sources of Divine Revelation was introduced — as a testing ground, I suspect, for what became the most controversial document of the Second Vatican Council. Interest heightened and there was less time for leisure. After all, the study, understanding and interpretation of the sacred writings and sayings was an important facet of every bishop's life. Late afternoon and evening lectures by experts in scriptural studies became necessary for most of us because our knowledge in that area went back to seminary days.

Just six general meetings during the first session of the Council were devoted to the subject of Divine Revelation, and so hostile became the debates that the Pope had to intervene. At our 24th general session a "straw vote" was called for. As a result, the preliminary schema on Divine Revelation prepared by the already overburdened Theological Commission was withdrawn, and Pope John XXIII was obliged to set up a special commission to revise the document.

Liturgy

The shape of the liturgy prior to Vatican II was fixed, rubrical and clerically dominated. Essentially, what the Constitution on the Sacred Liturgy did was to move away from the rigidity of several centuries of strict rubrics to a liturgy that allowed for variety, option and flexibility. It seriously encouraged the participation and the involvement of the worshipping community. It was a watershed document that was later implemented with some 25 post-conciliar decrees. Most of these covered all of the rites, from the consecration of bishops to the baptism of children. Key phrases like, "to impart an ever increasing vigor to the Christian life of the faithful . . . to adapt more closely to the needs of our age . . . to promote union among all those who believe in Christ," were at the heart of the adaptation of the sacraments that characterized these decrees.

There were seven schemata sent to the bishops of the world during the summer of 1962 in preparation for the opening of the Council on October 11. Of these, the draft document on the liturgy was the best presented to the Fathers of Vatican II for their discussion. The document was a tribute to the excellent work of the members of the Preparatory Commission. Among those members were two Americans: Father Frederick McManus of Catholic University in Washington, D.C., probably the best exponent of that subject in the United States; and Archbishop Paul Hallinan of Atlanta, Georgia, who represented the American bishops on that commission.

Fifteen general meetings of the Council were devoted to the liturgy schema, the only document not to be rejected or returned for complete revision. Again, this reflected not only the nature of the good preparation that went into that document, but also the vigorous work of the liturgical movement that had been active in Europe and America for almost fifty years. Serious scholars, with pastoral instincts — many of whom became members of the Preparatory Commission as well as periti at the Council — had made their views known long before the bishops got to Rome. Any serious reader of Church literature prior to the Council could not have avoided the movement for change in the liturgy.

The conciliar debates, known officially as interventions, best illustrate how the reform of the liturgy came about. There were more than 350 oral interventions and close to 1000 written proposals for change.

The opening salvo was the use of other languages than Latin in the celebration of the Eucharist. The use of the vernacular quickly became the rallying point (as it still is today) for those who were determined to adapt the Church's practice to meet the problems of a modern world. The question of the use of the vernacular also became a bone of contention for those who were determined to ignore a new and emerging Church no longer European, or Western or steeped in a juridical tradition.

I vividly recall the bearded and stately figure of the Melkite Patriarch of ancient Antioch, Maximos IV Saigh, whose intervention in favor of the vernacular brought the bishops to their feet. In exquisite French he pleaded with the Fathers of the Council that, even though the schema under discussion only concerned the Roman rite, as a prelate from the Eastern Church he had great interest in the liturgical movement in the Latin Church. He was especially disturbed about a phrase in the preliminary text that he considered abnormal for those in the Eastern tradition: "latinae linguae usu in liturgia occidentali servetur" (The use of Latin in the Western liturgies is to be maintained). The Patriarch went on to say that:

> It seems to me that the almost absolute value which this attempts to give to Latin in the liturgy, both in the teaching and in the administration of the Latin Church, is a sign of something which, to the Eastern Church is sufficiently abnormal. Christ, after all, talked in the language of His contemporaries. It was also in Aramaic that He offered the first sacrifice of the eucharist, in a language understood by all the people who heard Him. The Apostles and the Disciples did the same. It would never have occurred to them that, in a Christian assembly, the celebrant should deliver the scriptural lessons, or sing the psalms, or preach, or break bread, in a language other than that of the gathered faithful. St. Paul even tells us quite explicitly: "If thou dost pronounce a blessing in this spiritual fashion [that is to say, speaking an incomprehensible language], how can one who takes his place among the uninstructed say Amen to thy thanksgiving? He cannot tell what thou art saying. Thou, true enough, art duly giving thanks, but the other's faith is not strengthened. . . In the church, I would rather speak five words which my mind utters for your instruction, than ten thousand in a strange tongue" (1 Cor 14:16-19). All the reasons quoted in favor of keeping Latin untouched — a liturgical but dead language — must give way before this clear, sound and precise reasoning of the Apostle.
>
> In other respects, the Roman Church as well used Greek in her liturgy up to the third century, because it was the language used by the faithful of those times. And if then she started to abandon Greek in favor of Latin, it is precisely because Latin had become the language of the faithful. Why should the same principle not apply today?[1]

The gracious and gentle Eugene Cardinal Tisserant, head of the Vatican Library, rose in support of the Patriarch of Antioch and in a French-accented Latin, sometimes difficult to understand, emphasized that Latin was not the only liturgical language. Hebrew and Greek were also used by the original Christians. The Cardinal also reminded the bishops that certain Slavic languages, as well as Chinese, had been recognized by the Congregation of Rites in Rome as permissible liturgical languages.

A rather thorny question that came up during the early discussions on changes in the liturgy involved the source and authority that would regulate those changes. Cardinal Meyer of Chicago probably voiced the concern of most bishops when he objected to the proposal that a National Liturgical Commission become the responsible agency. He felt this to be an infringement on the authority of the local bishop, who, in his own diocese, should always be the moderator of pastoral liturgical action under the supervision of the Holy See and not of some national body. The Cardinal, however, approved such commissions as resource and study bodies for the bishops of a particular country. This has, for the most part, become the practice in many countries. In the United States, for instance, the local bishop might propose a change in the liturgy to the National Conference of Catholic Bishops, which in turn would ask its own liturgical commission to study the proposal in terms of its impact on the entire country. Were the conference of bishops to approve the change, the proposal would then be sent to Rome for adjudication.

The humility and prudence of Cardinal Meyer were disarming. When he spoke again a few days later, his words carried even more weight. His proposal that the liturgy of the hours (the breviary, which the priest is obliged to pray every day) be translated into the vernacular and that the priest not be obliged to read it at fixed hours, won the day. Changes for the more prayerful recitation of the daily breviary was one of the subjects many bishops reacted to when asked about an agenda for Vatican II. After all, the "office," as priests refer to it, was in need of reform. Its history, composition and order stemmed from practices in the monasteries, where the day was more easily regulated than that of a busy diocesan priest. And praying in Latin, for many priests who did not know the language, was a hindrance.

The changes in the liturgy of the hours, prompted by Cardinal Meyer's intervention, made its recitation less of a burden. They oriented the daily and obligatory prayers of the priest toward supporting and strengthening his spiritual life.

Communion under both species (bread and wine), a practice long in vogue in the Eastern Churches, engendered some heated debates. Although the subject was mentioned only once in the draft schema on the liturgy which we received earlier, there was unexpected opposition to the idea. And on the heels of that proposal, the question of concelebration of the Mass by groups of priests added fuel to the fire. This was treated in a more direct manner in the schema, and is another common practice in the Churches of the East. I remember distinctly that day when Cardinal Leger of Canada rose in support of both ideas to be greeted with the response of the head of the Holy Office, the inimitable Cardinal Ottaviani: "Are you Fathers planning a revolution?"

One of Cardinal Ottaviani's former students, a peritus at the Council, lived with us at the "Chicago House." We asked our fellow Chicagoan what the Cardinal was so concerned about. Father's reply was intuitive. He often visited the Cardinal at the orphanage His Eminence supported and said: "Well, he thinks there are too many changes going on and that the liturgy is being watered down; becoming too Protestant. Concelebration will make the Mass a big production unless it is strictly controlled."

It was always interesting to attend the press panel after discussions that generated some heat within the walls of St. Peter's. Inevitably, the press got wind of disagreements and was anxious to play these up. The one on communion under both species did bring up in the Council hall the matter of hygiene. A reporter mentioned this, but amid laughter an American expert on the liturgy reminded him of the potency of alcohol to kill any germs. Word also got out about the altar being turned around and the priest being forced to face the people. After some banter about his now being forced to "provide a saving face," being clean-shaven and the like, a missionary bishop in the audience spoke up in a more serious tone to remind the panel that, "No one who invites guests to supper turns his back on them."

Speaking in the name of the Dutch episcopate, Bishop Willem Bekkers probably gave the best and shortest summary of the discussion on the liturgy schema. He felt:

> That while the schema was not perfect it embodied the substance of what was necessary for a revival, in the hearts of the faithful, of the mystery-laden life of grace in Christ through a meaningful attendance at Mass and participation in the sacraments. On the prerogatives of bishops in these matters, it certainly was the Holy Father's right and duty to reserve certain powers to himself in dealing with individual dioceses or the whole Church. But as successors to the Apostles, the bishops possessed sufficient powers in these matters even though at present they were not exercising them out of deference and loyalty to the Holy See. [2]

Revelation

Prior to Vatican II, the Bible was interpreted quite literally and Scripture texts were uncritically used to support the Church's doctrinal teachings. Basically, ever since the Council of Trent, the view was held that Scripture (the written word) and Tradition (the teachings and practices of the Church through the ages) are two separate sources of Divine Revelation. Scripture scholars and theologians were concerned about this. For decades, they tried to explain that the biblical writers did not have, nor could they have had later Church teachings, traditions and customs in mind when they wrote.

The very essence of the long debates over the Dogmatic Constitution on Divine Revelation can therefore be traced to the problem of how the Sacred Scriptures were used and interpreted and applied to the Church's teachings. There were those who were anxious to preserve the scholastic method of reading and applying Holy Writ, and who felt that the Bible should not be tampered with. This was the impression the Council Fathers received when the first draft of the schema on Revelation was presented to them by the Theological Commission of the Council. And they were correct. Not only was the pastoral aspect of Revelation missing, but the schema seemed to be oriented toward the condemnation of errors or, at least, a subtle refutation of the newer doctrines coming out of biblical research.

Many of the bishops who came to Rome for the Council were well aware of the opposition to modern biblical scholarship on the part of some Roman curial officials. Many were familiar with Pope Pius XII's encyclical, *Divino Afflante Spiritu*, which actually opened the doors to the new methods of interpreting Sacred Scripture. This knowledge and the presence of a good number of biblical scholars who acted as periti to their bishops had great impact in turning about the schema on the sources of Revelation.

But before there was to be that turning about, the bishops had to come to an understanding of the sources of Revelation, of the new views of the role that tradition has in interpreting the sacred texts and the new look this is giving to Christian beliefs. They needed to have a clearer understanding of the theological problems that earlier in the century brought about the so-called Modernist crisis in the Church because of the application of critical historical methods to the interpretation of Scripture. Many of them remembered that as priests and bishops they once had to take an oath against Modernism.

And so, as in the case of the liturgical movement, a new appreciation of the method of God's Revelation to man had become a reality within the Church in the decades before the Council. The

Council needed to take this up, to deepen it and extend it to the whole Church.

The controversy which dogged the Dogmatic Constitution on Divine Revelation took on various forms of expression and brought about, as I observed earlier, the personal intervention of the Pope and his request that a new schema be prepared by a mixed commission of theologians and Scripture scholars.

Notes which I preserved and quotes which I had written on the margins of the preparatory draft of the schema on Revelation reveal the depth of the dissatisfaction of the bishops with the document presented by the Theological Commission. One such note, in red ink no less, says: "The original sin of the Council lay in the defective work of the Preparatory Commission." I learned later, in going through Cardinal Meyer's archives in preparation for this work, that the fault was not in the persons but in the methods used by those responsible for bringing the members of the commission together. For instance, meetings were held without prior notice or with delayed notice to members, especially those versed in scriptural studies.

Other notes I made, speak of the grave faults of the schema from an ecumenical point. I recall Bishop Emile De Smedt's intervention on this subject. Some said that his speech, which was greeted with sustained applause, turned the tide in favor of a completely new document. In substance he felt that unless the nature of the schema on Revelation was changed, the Council would be responsible for destroying a great and immense hope, the hope of those who, "like Pope John XXIII, are waiting in prayer and fasting for an important and significant step in the direction of fraternal unity." Another prelate, whose name I neglected to insert in my notes said: "We should be thinking of our separated brethren who have a great love and veneration for the Word of God."

It is probably fair to say that many of us bishops were not familiar with the reasons why a number of the Council Fathers made references to the ecumenical implications of the schema on

Revelation. I noticed that most of those who brought up the subject were Scripture scholars. Father George Tavard, a theologian and a peritus at the Council, in a post-Vatican II survey of the theological background of the Council, made this astute observation:

> Most of the theologians of our contemporary renewal have been, at one time or another, involved in the ecumenical movement. There has been a cross-fertilization of Catholic and Protestant thought, not only at the level of biblical scholarship, but also at that of theological reflection. This is indeed a remarkable progress on the attitude of former days, when Protestant theologies were hardly considered to belong among Christian theologies. But this is not simply the result of reading Protestant authors. It is in the first place the logical outcome of the advance of ecclesiological studies in Catholic theology.[3]

The opposition of the Jesuit, Augustin Cardinal Bea, considered to be the most respected Scripture scholar in the world, was profound. His intervention on the ecumenical aspect of the schema deeply impressed the bishops when he said that:

> The schema does not correspond to the purposes which the Pope determined for the Council, which should reflect a concern for the pastoral ministry and unity.[4]

Many of us suspected that the 82-year-old Cardinal, though feeble looking, but now aroused, was reflecting the sentiments of Pope John XXIII and the powerful words the Pope used in his opening address to the Council on October 11, 1962. The Pope had insisted that:

> Illuminated by the light of this Council, the Church — we confidently trust—will become greater in spiritual riches and, gaining the strength of new energies therefrom, She will look to the future without fear. In fact, by bringing herself up to date where required, and by the wise organization of mutual cooperation, the Church will make men, families and peoples really turn their minds

to heavenly things . . . the Christian, Catholic and apostolic spirit of the whole world expects a step forward toward a doctrinal penetration and a formation of consciences in faithful and perfect conformity to the authentic doctrine which, however, should be studied and expounded through the methods of research and through the literary forms of modern thought. The substance of the ancient doctrine of the Deposit of Faith is one thing, and the way in which it is presented is another. And it is the latter that must be taken into great consideration, with patience if necessary, everything being measured in the forms and proportions of a *magisterium* which is predominantly pastoral in character.[5]

I had personal confirmation of this from Cardinal Meyer, a member with Bea of the newly formed Mixed Commission, who told us at dinner one evening that, "after all, there was that personal hand-written letter the Pope sent Cardinal Bea in which he urged that the Cardinal continue his efforts that 'all may be one in the Blood of Christ.' "

After the long and hard debates on the sources of Revelation, two other critical points were raised before the document won the final approval of the Council Fathers: the question of a more detailed account of the "inerrancy" of Sacred Scripture (that is, its truth and how that is to be taught), as well as that of the form in which the historicity of the Gospels was to be anchored in the text of the Constitution.

Bishop Butler in his book, *The Theology of Vatican II*, made this observation regarding the meaning of inerrancy in our day:

But for an age as conscious as our own of the extremely human and contingent character of literary records, an age so suspicious of miraculous claims and so sensitive to the approximative character of human evidence, the notion of inspiration, especially when it is spelt out in terms of "inerrancy," is hardly marketable at all. Of this difficulty some, but not all, of the Council Fathers were anxiously aware.[6]

The question of the literary forms in which the historicity of the Gospels were to be interpreted, was also a prolonged matter of debate. Cardinal Ruffini "blasted" the new freedom allowed Scripture scholars and repeated his condemnation that:

> The employment of literary forms in biblical exegesis was tantamount to admitting that the Church had not understood the Scriptures until modern times.[7]

In this respect, the Cardinal from Palermo was actually repeating his explicit criticism of Pope Pius XII's encyclical *Divino Afflante Spiritu*, for which he had been publicly challenged before the start of the Council.[8]

Again, the then Abbot Butler, of Downside, England, summed up the difficulty on both sides of the argument and attempted to allay the fears of the minority by assuring them that the historicity of Divine Revelation was not in jeopardy. Rather, the apologetic approach of previous Catholic scholarship could now be supplemented by a wider and more factual consideration of the biblical witness to God's Word. "We do not want," the Abbot said, "the childish comfort of averting our gaze from the truth, but a truly critical scholarship which will enable us to enter into dialogue with non-Catholic scholars."[9]

Actually, what was happening prior to the Council (and more certainly after the Council) was that biblical scholarship had anticipated the "aggiornamento" or renewal, that Pope John XXIII had called for. Using the new discoveries in the archaeological, literary, and historical fields that relate to apostolic times, the Bible scholars hoped to arrive at a better appreciation of Our Lord's words and deeds. They did this by trying to analyze the context and the atmosphere in which events surrounding the life of Christ, His Apostles and the early Church occurred.

As is evident, therefore, the Council Fathers were subjected to a disorganized classroom on Sacred Scripture. In our case, as well as in the case of other national episcopal conferences, American ingenuity prevailed. The American bishops began a series of many meetings at their North American College in Rome, where biblical scholars like Passionist Father Barnabas Mary Ahern and Jesuit Father Francis McCool and others, filled our evenings with information and orientation. In addition, there were many opportunities to attend the lectures of noted Scripture scholars who either taught at the Roman schools or came to the Council as periti with their bishops.

Continued debate over the next six working congregations, as our meetings at St. Peter's were called, during November, 1962, proved even more decisive. The Benedictine Abbot Butler, now Auxiliary Bishop of Westminster, called those days, ''the central drama of the first session.''

The stellar figure in that drama turned out to be the learned Cardinal Meyer of Chicago. Although he sided with an open-door approach in general, and while he warned that tradition is broader in scope that the Bible, Cardinal Meyer emphasized that living tradition is not always free of human defects. It is subject to failings since the Church is still a pilgrim in the world. As examples of where this tradition has deviated from the ideal, he cited the exaggerated moralism of the past centuries, private pious practices which have grown away from the spirit of the liturgy, neglect of the Bible, and even the active discouragement of Bible reading among Catholics.[10]

But at the heart of it all, at the epicenter of the Dogmatic Constitution on Divine Revelation, was this Meyeran conclusion:

> This constitution has an importance far beyond its immediate significance. Dogmatists may argue whether Scripture and Tradition are one or two sources of Revelation, but that text we have now before us states clearly that together they constitute one sacred deposit of the Word of God through which the People of God in union with their shepherds, persevere in preserving, practicing and professing the faith.

Needless to say, the aula of St. Peter's that late morning of October 5, 1964, thundered with applause for a Cardinal from the United States, known as a Scripture scholar, whose deep thought and objectivity placed him in a limelight he found embarrassing — but for those who knew him, it was a limelight that was well deserved.

Since the Dogmatic Constitution on Divine Revelation deals with the very heart of Christian beliefs, it was and is considered by many as the most significant achievement of Vatican II. It opened up for Catholic scholars new methods of scriptural research, the application of new scientific biblical critiques and the overall opportunity to re-evaluate the Sacred Scriptures.

As for the concept of Tradition, which became the center, as I have observed, of much heated discussion, Father Barnabas Mary Ahern, the noted Scripture scholar and peritus to Cardinal Meyer of Chicago, made this refreshing analysis:

> Tradition is now presented as embracing the whole life of the Church, its teaching, its cult, its practice. God is always speaking to everyone in the Church through the truths of Revelation and through the illumination of His Holy Spirit; and the Church is always responding with a faith which can never fail. . . . This concept of tradition spells a new dignity for every Christian, giving him a full role to play in the perennially vital transmission of God's word to the world. This means, too, a new urgency for full Christian living, intelligent and wholehearted. Each man must realize that he is part of a living tradition. In his weakness he will always need the light and control of the Church's teaching authority. But what he himself is and lives by, his belief, his prayer, his conduct — all this enters into the Church's full tradition. Each Christian is a living echo of the voice of God.[11]

Out of the controversy that surrounded the Dogmatic Constitution on Divine Revelation came much that is positive. This is true in a special way of the debate that involved Tradition as a source of Revelation. New roles for the laity in the Church stand out in this document. It is clear that Revelation as it exists stems from the Tradition of the living Christian communities at the outset of the Christian era, and in Scripture which was born of this Tradition. Through these two the Church finds God in Revelation. The Constitution endorses that concept this way:

> Now what was handed on by the Apostles includes everything which contributes to the holiness of life, and the increase in faith of the People of God; and so the Church, in her teaching, life, and worship, perpetuates and hands on to all generations all that she herself is, all that she believes . . . This happens through the contemplation and study made by believers, who treasure these things in their hearts (cf. Lk 2:19, 51), through the intimate understanding of spiritual things they experience, and through the preaching of those who have received through episcopal succession the sure gift of truth (#8).

That is a good description of the "development of dogma," and it was precisely this development of Tradition as a source of Revelation that brought about much of the debate during the third session of Vatican II. Father Barnabas Mary Ahern, in his summary of the Dogmatic Constitution on Divine Revelation, makes this practical application of the development of tradition:

> It is hardly needful to say what this means for the apostolate of the laity. Previously our laity have been called the "hands of the Church," reaching into areas where otherwise the Church's teaching would have no influence. The schema shows the profound reason why the laity are so necessary and how it is possible for them to perform so great a task. They, like everyone else in the Church, are living voices of tradition. In their lives other men hear God speaking and God's Son responding. For the world at large, that world of men who know nothing of Pope or bishop or priest, the voice of God will be heard chiefly through its resonant echo in the lives of our Catholic laity.[12]

If I might paraphrase Father Ahern's words, God made His creatures partners in the whole process of revelation.

And there is this refreshing viewpoint of the present head of the Sacred Congregation for the Doctrine of the Faith, Joseph Cardinal Ratzinger:

> In the process of assimilating what is really rational and in rejecting what only seems to be rational, the whole Church has to play a part. This process cannot be carried out in every detail by an isolated Magisterium, with oracular infallibility. The life and suffering of Christians who profess their faith in the midst of their times has just as important a part to play as the thinking and questioning of the learned, which would have a hollow ring without the backing of Christian existence, which learns to discern spirits in the travail of everyday life. [13]

FOOTNOTES

(For full citations of sources, please see the Bibliography)

1. Rynne, p. 103.
2. Ibid., p. 110.
3. Tavard, p. 37.
4. Wenger, p. 77.
5. Rynne, pp. 264, 268.
6. Butler, p. 41.
7. Rynne, *Third Session*, p. 43.
8. Rynne, pp. 54-55.
9. Butler, p. 47.
10. *Council Daybook*, Vol. 2, p. 83.
11. Ibid., Vol. 2, pp. 139-140.
12. Ibid., p. 140.
13. Ratzinger, p. 83.

VII.

Ministry

The Church is at the center of our lives. When we think of faith, of God, of working out our salvation, we think of the Church. Our Catholic identity is with the Church, but it is also with Jesus Christ. That vital link between Christ and His Church exists because the Church issues forth from Christ and is identified with His person and work. There are among us those who choose to be associated with Christ's person and His work. Some of us are called to the ordained ministry; others, through baptism and confirmation, not only participate in the general priesthood of Christ, but are called to a non-sacramental ministry. St. Thomas Aquinas started it all when he said that, "orders is a sacrament, ministry is not." The text on ministries from the Dogmatic Constitution on the Church is prophetic:

> It is not only through the sacraments and Church ministries that the same Holy Spirit sanctifies and leads the People of God and enriches it with virtues . . . He distributes special graces among the faithful of every rank. By these gifts He makes them fit and ready to undertake the various tasks or offices advantageous for the renewal and upbuilding of the Church (#12).

When the Second Vatican Council articulated a new theology of the Church as the People of God, and a new understanding of the use of authority, a problem faced contemporary theologians in their research on ministry: the specific difference between ordained ministry and the priesthood of the laity.

It must be admitted that the diversities of ministries that came about since the end of Vatican II developed more quickly than reflection on them or clarification between them. The increasing number of lay people participating in the ministerial life of the Church presents a challenge that touches on the role of the priest and the "character" of the sacrament of orders. Understandably, priests are haunted by what today appears to be a diminishment of their ministry to that of a "sacramental functionary."

Hopefully, the Synod of Bishops scheduled for the Fall of 1987, designed to discuss "The Vocation and Mission of the Laity in the Church," will clarify the situation. A theology of lay ministry in the Church, worthy of the directives that came out of Vatican II, still needs to be written.

The question of vocation to ministry is primordial to what Christianity is all about. I propose to discuss in this chapter the priesthood, that special calling through the sacrament of orders to serve the People of God, and the ministry of the laity that emerges from the call of all Christians to continue Christ's redemptive mission to the world. Vatican II emphasized (in its documents on the priesthood and the laity) that vocation, expressed in a particular ministry, involves a specialization that comes out of the development of a particular charism. Any charism or call, therefore, comes from the Spirit and flows from each person's engagement with the Lord Jesus. I can't imagine a more responsible, more satisfying and effective call than that of making Jesus present to others, through priesthood, or through sharing in the ever-present, loving, merciful and compassionate service of the laity. As the Dogmatic Constitution on the Church states:

> Now, the laity are called in a special way to make the Church present and operative in those places and circumstances where only through them can she become the salt of the earth (#33).

The Priesthood

The Decree on the Ministry and Life of Priests is another example of a document that came out of the Second Vatican Council by the express wish of the bishops. After all, Pope John XXIII did ask us, after he announced the calling of a Council, for ideas or subject matter for such a gathering of the world's bishops. It is known that the bishops listed the priesthood as a priority for discussion. Most bishops therefore, like myself, came to the Council eager for a document that would relate directly to those who were our closest collaborators. But quick and grave was our disappointment when, during discussion of article twenty of the schema on the Church, our priests were given short shrift. The text devoted nine pages to the episcopate, seven pages to the laity and just half of one page to the priesthood. In Chapter V, I discussed the vicissitudes of the schema that finally became the Decree on the Life and Ministry of Priests.

This chapter will be partly devoted to considering the priesthood as ministry, especially in those aspects that distinguish the priest from the lay person as we envisioned his role in our discussions at the Council.

Perhaps the most important aspect that concerned us at the Council was in how the priest differs from others among the People of God because of his consecration and mission. And it was the absence of this concept that generated disappointment among us bishops with the first schema on the priesthood presented to us. Even the completed Decree in its very title ignores this important fact. Article 1 emphasizes not the consecration and sanctity which is part of the priest's mission, but his ministry and function within the Church. That article even neglects to build on the beautiful language of article 28 of the Dogmatic Constitution on the Church which states:

Christ, whom the Father sanctified and sent into the world (Jn 10:36) has, through His apostles, made their successors, the bishops, partakers of His consecration and His mission. These in their turn have legitimately handed on to different individuals in the Church various degrees of participation in this ministry. Thus the divinely established ecclesiastical ministry is exercised on different levels by those who from antiquity have been called bishops, priests, and deacons.

When discussion on the twelve guiding principles on the life and ministry of priests of the schema *De Sacerdotibus* was opened for discussion at the third session, Cardinal Meyer of Chicago spoke to us at dinner one evening about the weakness of the document. His love for the priesthood was well known and he was determined to speak out. On October 13, 1964, as soon as Archbishop Marty of Rheims, secretary for the commission responsible for the schema on priests, finished presenting those "guiding principles," Cardinal Meyer was the first to speak and literally "hit the nail on the head" with these words:

> In all sincerity, I should confess that this schema of propositions is not very satisfactory because proper and fuller discussion is not given to what is of such great importance, as was done in the schema on "The Pastoral Duties of Bishops," and in the schema "On the Apostolate of the Laity."
>
> Therefore, I should like something said, at least in the preface, about the dignity, the necessity and the high mission of the priest in the whole complex of the Church's mission. It is true that the preface, as it now reads, briefly recalls what is said of priests in the schema, De Ecclesia. But these things should be emphasized at greater length under the pastoral aspect.
>
> It is hard for me to understand why, after the preface, a sudden transition is made to "conversation of priests with laity." It is true that the priest is appointed for men, but in those things which are of God. Let him, therefore, be a man of God before he is a man among men. [1]

Cardinal Meyer was critical of the first of those twelve propositions on the priesthood, in which it was implied that the priest is primarily a member of the Christian community and must behave like a brother among brothers. He was to be above all an example of those qualities that are so important in all human relationships.

On the eve of our departure for home, at the end of the third session of the Council, a new schema was given us on the priesthood, a 44-page brochure on "The Life and Ministry of Priests" that we were to study and to send written comments on to the General Secretary by the end of the following January.

It is interesting to note that only 157 Council Fathers sent in their observations on the brochure. Despite its title, the brochure was directed not so much to the life of the priest (about which many bishops intervened), but to his ministry. It thus gave the impression that the priest's life must be determined by the requirements of his ministry and not vice versa.

On the other hand, the concept of the presbyterate in the words of John 10:36 stood out in that brochure and this is what most of the responding bishops reacted to. This was so much the case, that when we returned to Rome for the fourth session of the Council, the second version of the decree on the life and ministry of priests contained more of what the bishops were looking for in such a document. For instance, the nature of the presbyterate was emphasized within the framework of the universal mission of the Church, and the nature of the official priesthood was explained in distinction to the general priesthood of all the faithful on the one hand, and to the episcopate on the other.

It should be kept in mind that the very title of the final version of the decree on the priesthood, *Prebyterorum Ordinis* has its origin in the New Testament word, "presbyter" as the second of the hierarchical ladder that includes bishops and deacons. The word was also frequently used by the early Fathers of the Church. Irenaeus, in his treatise *Against Heresies*, states that:

We must listen to the presbyters in the Church; they are the successors of the apostles. And with the succession in the episcopate they
have received the certain charism of truth according to the Father's
pleasure.[2]

Who then was this "presbyter" the bishops were so interested
in, this man consecrated? In the words of John 10:36, he is "The
one sanctified and sent into the world by the Father." He is the
"other Christ" set apart by God to fulfill His mandate and mission.
He serves the people committed to him so that he can more properly
imitate the perfection of Him whose part he takes. He heals the
weaknesses of the human flesh because of the holiness of Him
whom he follows, who has become for our sake, "such a high
priest, holy, innocent, undefiled, set apart from sinners" (Heb
7:26).

Most of us bishops from the very beginning of the Council were
looking for just such a theological dissertation on the nature of the
priesthood, at least to the same extent that the episcopal office was
handled in the Dogmatic Constitution on the Church. Had that been
done, perhaps there would be less confusion today on the role of the
ordained ministry in relation to the proliferation of the non-
ordained who serve the Church so admirably.

The commission in charge of the schema on the priesthood,
however, had other ideas. It was their position that it would be
interfering with the work of the Commission on Doctrine. This
latter group was busy refining the special chapter on the hierarchy
for the Dogmatic Constitution on the Church, in which some
consideration of the priesthood would be given. Then again, work
was going on with other documents that would refer to the priesthood: the Constitution on the Sacred Liturgy, the Decree on the
Bishop's Pastoral Office in the Church, and the Decree on Priestly
Formation.

On October 13, 1965, exactly two years after the first schema
on the priesthood was introduced amid so much controversy, what
would become the final draft of the document on the priesthood

was brought to the floor of St. Peter's. It came with an instruction from Pope Paul VI that any debate on the subject of priestly celibacy would not be appropriate.

It was known that a good number of Council Fathers had asked for an exposition of the foundation of the Church's doctrine on, and of the appropriateness of, priestly celibacy. When the question of priestly celibacy (article 16) was addressed, the comments by the Fathers were more numerous than on any other question in the schema on the priesthood. A final tally of the voting on November 12 and 13, 1965, revealed that 187 of the *modi* (suggestions for changes) were related to the title of the document, 43 on its general structure, 1331 on the celibacy question, 972 regarding aids priests need to enhance their spiritual lives, and 762 involving their relationship to one another.

The Pope's determination to uphold the law of celibacy was evident in a letter he had asked Cardinal Tisserant, Dean of the Sacred College of Cardinals, to read to the Council Fathers:

> Public debate is not opportune on this subject which is so important and which demands such profound prudence. Furthermore, it is our intention not only to maintain this ancient, sacred and providential law with all the force of which we are capable, but also to reinforce its observance, calling on priests of the Latin Church to recognize anew the causes and reasons why today, especially today, the law must be considered most suitable. Through it priests are able to concentrate all their love completely to Christ and to dedicate themselves exclusively and generously to service of the Church and souls.[3]

The Second Vatican Council was winding down toward its conclusion in October 1965 with the last document to be debated, that on priestly life and ministry. Anticipation ran high, not only of the prospects of returning home, but with the conviction that much was accomplished. Day after day, completed schemata were presented to the bishops, voted on and passed on to the Holy Father for

promulgation. Between October and December 8, 1965, eleven of
the sixteen documents of Vatican II were approved by the Pope.
Among the last three were the Decree on the Ministry and Life of
Priests, but not without this bit of humor.

A bishop dared in the last hours to suggest that the title of the
decree be changed to that of, ''The Holiness of Priests.'' A
frustrated confrere rose to ask if a ''diocesan priest could be said to
live in a state of holiness as do religious priests?'' He felt that the
text about to be promulgated implied that such a state was impossi-
ble for diocesan priests. Another prelate broke the silence that
ensued with the observation that most of the bishops at Vatican II
came from the ranks of the diocesan clergy.

A note I appended to the margin of the schema before me that
day, apparently a quote from a lecture I had attended, said:

> Priestly holiness is not seen within the context of the holiness of the
> People of God. The theme of what a man is bound to be as a priest
> obscures the theme of what he is bound to be as a Christian.

And then I noted the observation:

> After all, the fifth chapter of De Ecclesia [i.e., *Lumen Gentium*, the
> Dogmatic Constitution on the Church] does speak of ''The Call of
> the Whole Church to Holiness.''

A unique highlight of the Decree on the Ministry and Life of
Priests was the stress on the obligation of preaching. When we
were discussing chapter 2 of the decree, the bishops became very
interested in the explanation of the three priestly functions — that
of teaching, governing, and sanctifying. What became significant
was footnote 4 to article 1 of the decree which now reads:

> From the very outset there is mention of the priest's mission and the
> threefold ministry by which he discharges this mission: he serves
> Christ the Teacher (ministry of the Word), Christ the Priest
> (ministry of the sacraments and the Eucharist), Christ the King
> (ministry of ruling the People of God). This is developed in Ch. 2.

What is interesting to note about this threefold role of the priest's mission is the order in which those offices are listed. This is not without significance and importance, especially today when there is so much confusion and misunderstanding about the role of the minister (ministry) and priest (priesthood). The commission to preach comes first, it puts faith into words.

Bishops were not the only speakers allowed the floor of the Council. In the fall of 1964, Pope Paul VI saw fit to invite pastors from throughout the world to be on hand for discussion of the schema on priestly life and ministry. Four Americans were chosen. Representing these pastors, a Monsignor Thomas Falls of Philadelphia had this to say about the schema:

> We pastors are very pleased with the schema. We are pleased with the clear distinction made between the common priesthood of the laity and the ministerial priesthood of priests. We are also pleased with the strong recommendation that priests live a community life . . . that priests celebrate Mass daily . . . that priests be given proper sustenance . . . we believe that the schema should spell out in detail the concrete obligations of the bishop to guarantee a decent living wage to every priest in his diocese . . . Finally, we are pleased with what has been said on the question of clerical celibacy which we feel must be observed, with all due reverence to our brothers of the Oriental Church.[4]

The image of the priest today is, therefore, that of a consecrated person who participates in the mission of Christ in a very special way. He does so in a distinct way, of course, from the lay person — who by virtue of baptism and confirmation also participates in Christ's priesthood.

However, this image of the priest also needs to be framed in this bit of realism best expressed, during one of our discussions on the holiness required of the priest, by the youthful Cardinal Doepfner of Munich, Germany:

The day's first speaker, Julius Cardinal Doepfner of Munich, Germany, pointed out that the text mentions the authority relationship between bishops and priests 14 times, while referring to the importance of the Eucharist only five times. He said priests might justly rankle at the reference to them as ''a precious spiritual crown for the bishop,'' even though the words come from St. Ignatius, martyr.

Not only the public aspects of a priest's life should be emphasized, he said, such as the celebration of Mass and the administration of the sacraments, but also his personal priestly life. The text should be ''more sober and accurate'' and less like a spiritual reading, which is proper in a pious book but out of place in a council document. The recognition of pastoral sanctity as distinct from sanctity for Religious should be developed. A pastoral theology should also be developed which recognizes a priest's solitude and isolation in the modern world, he stated.[5]

The People of God

> But you are a chosen race, a royal priesthood, a holy nation, a people claimed by God for his own . . . you are now the people of God (1 P 2:9-10).

That title, ''The People of God,'' as footnote 27 to the beginning of chapter 2 of the Dogmatic Constitution on the Church emphasizes,

> met a profound desire of the Council to put greater emphasis on the human and communal side of the Church, rather than on the institutional and hierarchical aspects which have sometimes been overstressed in the past for polemical reasons.

Little did the bishops realize, however, when trying to develop this concept, that there would come about not only a pluralism of ministries but virtually a literal interpretation of such phrases as ''made a kingdom and priests to God his Father'' (Rv 1:6, quoted in the Dogmatic Constitution on the Church, #10). The same could be said of these phrases from the same article of that document:

> The baptized, by regeneration and the anointing of the Holy Spirit, are consecrated into a spiritual house and a holy priesthood.

> Though they differ from one another in essence and not only in degree, the common priesthood of the faithful and the ministerial or hierarchical priesthood are nonetheless interrelated. Each of them in its own special way is a participation in the one priesthood of Christ.

Granted, all of these phrases provide a new foundation for what the bishops wanted to emphasize, namely the fundamental equality of all Christians in the sight of God. They do not, however — if one studies carefully the footnotes in the Dogmatic Constitution on the Church — diminish the role of those who have received the divine call to serve the People of God.

I believe that the council Fathers really exercised a prophetic vision when they provided for the laity not only new roles but a new dignity in the economy of salvation. Yet, what has resulted, in terms of the new ministries, needs to become a part of the Church's life and practice. This is something the Council Fathers did not think of. In reality, a new theology of ministry in the Church must be built on the foundation provided by the bishops of Vatican II.

We have already greatly benefited from the whole-hearted welcome that our formerly clerically dominated Church has given a laity that is eager—and in many instances, well-prepared—to serve the mission of Christ on earth. Here in the United States particularly, the laity have come of age. As Eugene Kennedy puts it:

> Today's lay people constitute a new and formidable presence in the Church. The clergy cannot ignore or handle them the way they did in the past.[6]

In other words, the Church in the United States is benefiting today from the well-prepared graduates of its Catholic educational

system, the rising number of lay people dedicated to their faith and
anxious to serve it, and a Catholic laity that possesses a theological
sophistication that needs to be reckoned with.

Today, a committed laity are a consolation and encouragement
to their bishops and priests. They are living proof that the bishops
of Vatican II — though they may not have foreseen those changing
roles in ministry that came with the lessening number of priests and
religious — were indeed moved by the Holy Spirit in providing a
new vision of the Church. How practical then, are these statements
from just a few of the documents that came from the Council:

> Bishops, pastors of parishes, and other priests of both branches of
> the clergy should keep in mind that the right and duty to exercise the
> apostolate is common to all the faithful, both clergy and laity, and
> that the laity also have their own proper roles in building up the
> Church. For this reason, they should work fraternally with the laity
> in and for the Church and take special care of the lay persons
> engaged in apostolic works (Decree on the Apostolate of the Laity,
> #25).

> Priests should also confidently entrust to the laity duties in the
> service of the Church, allowing them freedom and room for action.
> In fact, on suitable occasions, they should invite them to undertake
> works on their own initiative (Decree on the Ministry and Life of
> Priests, #9).

> Pastors of souls must therefore realize that, when the liturgy is
> celebrated, more is required than the mere observance of the laws
> governing valid and licit celebration. It is their duty also to ensure
> that the faithful take part knowingly, actively, and fruitfully (Con-
> stitution on the Sacred Liturgy, #11).

In the early years after the Council, the laity, with the encouragement of their priests, put these texts into practice by participating more actively in the work of the Church. They volunteered their
services on diocesan and parish councils, on boards of education,
on financial, liturgical and ecumenical committees.

As the years went on they moved closer to the sanctuary as lectors, commentators, distributors of communion and ministers of hospitality (ushers).

Some became fully employed teachers in Catholic schools, replacing the religious who dominated that field for centuries. Others moved into the specialized area of religious education. Laity began to be seen as campus ministers, youth ministers and spiritual directors.

Encouraged by their pastors, some laity relied on pre-Vatican II models of ministry. They took on clerical apostolates that, before the Council, had been the province of priests and religious. Many of these new ecclesial ministries in the Church have been good and positive. But this is not what the Council Fathers really had in mind when, in defining episcopacy and priesthood in more pastoral terms, they also took steps to include the laity in the ministry of the Church.

We need to remember that the only hierarchical change made at Vatican II (outside the concept of collegiality, which is not of the essence of orders) was the restoration of the permanent diaconate. Even on this subject, the Council Fathers were divided. The established dioceses opposed the restoration, whereas the missionary bishops and those from the third world supported the idea.

As a Vatican II bishop I did not think (and I'm sure that I can include most of my confreres who went to Rome) that we would come to this paradox symptomatic of our times: that while we face real problems because of the shortage of priests and religious, we have the happy circumstance of the rising number of, and the improving relationship among, the many new lay ministries in the Church of our day.

I look at it this way: The fundamental assertion of the Council's Dogmatic Constitution on the Church is that the Church has been sent by Christ, just as Christ was sent by the Father. Ministry has its source in Jesus Christ and must, therefore, be a continuation of His ministry. It is His mission from the Father to all peoples that the

Church carries out. It was the manner in which this mission was to be carried out, and by whom, that interested the Council Fathers of Vatican II.

Bishop John Wright of Pittsburgh, chairman of the sub-commission responsible for the Decree on the Apostolate of the Laity, and representing some 50 other American bishops, expressed that concept best in his intervention:

> The Decree on the Apostolate of the Laity recognizes un-equivocally that the *apostolate of the laity*, in its authentic sense, is a participation *in the saving mission of the Church*; that the priestly work of the laity, as laity, should be thus *directly* defined in terms of the work of the Church itself.[7]

And so it came about that the very controversial and highly publicized decision about episcopal collegiality (which I discussed in Chapter VI) had to find its analogous application in the diocese and the parish and consequently with the laity. Article 37 of the Dogmatic Constitution on the Church provides the foundation in these words:

> Let sacred pastors recognize and promote the dignity as well as the responsibility of the layman in the Church. Let them willingly make use of his prudent advice. Let them confidently assign duties to him in the service of the Church, allowing him freedom and room for action.

Again, the footnote (176) to that article stresses the "right" of the layperson to an active role in the Church. It is interesting that the new Code of Canon Law not only repeats much of the language of the article verbatim, but stresses again and again, in fifteen canons, the "rights" and "new responsibilities" of the laity in the work of the Church.

The use of the word "right" or "rights" on the part of the laity in the Church was probably inspired by an American bishop who spoke on this concept very early in our discussion on shared responsibility. Bishop Charles Greco of Alexandria, Louisiana stressed not only the layperson's obligation to participate in the salvific mission of the Church, but went on to say that:

> Thus it seems best to me that the constitution of this section (page nine, line eight), after it has discerned the obligation and duty, affirm the right of laymen to cooperate in religious works with these words: "And so these people (laymen) have the *right* with their resources, actively and in their own way, to participate in the salvific work of the Church."[8]

But all of this was not easy to come by during our sessions at the Council. More than 700 interventions were made by the bishops to not only improve the text on the apostolate of the laity, but to build on the foundational design of the chapter on the laity in the Dogmatic Constitution on the Church.

One of the reasons I stress with Bishops Wright and Greco this matter of paricipation in the *salvific mission of the Church* is that, soon after the Council, there was much stress on lay participation in the temporal works of the Church. Although the Council Fathers did not exclude the idea of bishops and priests seeking lay expertise in governing the Church's temporal interests (cf. art. 37 of the Dogmatic Constitution on the Church, quoted above), too little attention was given the laity's spiritual mission.

As discussion on the role of the laity progressed, it became clearer that although they do not belong to the hierarchy, they share in the mission of the Church in order to sanctify the world from within. I remember an expression Pope John XXIII used in his book, *Journal of a Soul*: "we must infect the world with Christ."

Simply put, although the Council stressed "that a secular quality is proper and special to laymen," the lay person in his or her milieu has the particular responsibility of preaching the Christian message and witnessing to the world. Many of the Vatican II prelates dwelt so strongly on this that this wording was adopted:

> The lay apostolate, however, is a participation in the saving mission of the Church itself (Dogmatic Constitution on the Church, #33).

Prior to the Council, the stress was on lay participation in the hierarchical mission of the Church. But with the concept of all being a part of the People of God, the bishops adopted a new vocabulary in that same article when they said:

> Now, the laity are called in a special way to make the Church present and operative in those places and circumstances where only through them can she become the salt of the earth.

An interesting controversy that won the attention of the bishops one morning during the first weeks of our discussions centered on the problem of "individualism." This of course was a natural outcome of our debates on bringing about an application of the concept, "People of God," which we were struggling with for the first time. Were we one in Christ or were we divided as Christians? In just this area, internal to the Church — and without any thought of our separated brothers and sisters, whose condition we would have to face up to later — tempers flared.

There's a phrase I wrote on the margin of the schema we were considering one early morning, "the pastoral heresy of individualism" with an exclamation mark. Digging through notes that I saved, I discovered that the phrase was attributed to the versatile Coadjutor Bishop Arthur Elchinger of Strasbourg in France, who said:

> Too many Christians seek spiritual security and personal satisfaction in their reception of the sacraments without ever experiencing the practical consequences of incorporation into the Mystical Body of Christ. The danger of the heresy of individualism is besetting the laity, and also the clergy and the hierarchy. It is the task of this Council to find a remedy for this pastoral heresy.[9]

How true that phrase was, at least on the part of those Christians who sought the salvation of their own souls without concern for the souls of others. In the coffee bar that morning there was much comment. Some bishops who were members of religious orders thought that Bishop Elchinger was criticizing the contemplatives, those religious who shut themselves up from the world to devote all of their time to prayer. Others, like myself, shared the experiences we had with the indifferent Catholic, the church-going Sunday person, who neglected to apply the priest's sermon on love of neighbor during the rest of the week. One bishop with espresso in hand, remarked: "Certain prelates and priests are not themselves true witnesses of the gospel they preach." Another bishop mentioned a confrere who seldom, or with reluctance applied in his own diocese the decisions reached by his fellow bishops in conference. One of the bishops from England, known for his wit, said that, "Maybe those boys in the Curia here in Rome will begin to talk with us lesser lights."

By the way, it was about this time that Cardinal Suenens of Belgium proposed that women be invited as auditors to the Council. My notes indicate that he made this proposal after a bishop said something to the effect that, "It is a fact of history that some members of the laity have at times awakened a sleeping Church."

On the way to the Chicago House of Studies that morning for lunch, the three of us, Cardinal Meyer, Bishop O'Donnell and myself, shared our experiences. I recalled the coffee bar incidents. O'Donnell said that he ran into his friend Bishop Marcos McGrath of Panama, who elaborated on his intervention about the laity, that we treat them like little acolytes, that they are at the bottom of a clerical pyramid. The Cardinal must have been thinking about an intervention he was planning, because in his usual quiet and sagacious way he reminded us that everyone, called by baptism into the Church, is a sinner. I felt that we were put down and reminded of the word "charity."

Indeed, Cardinal Meyer's intervention on the People of God went like this:

In order that our schema may reach the hearts of men today — men who are burdened by a sense both of sin and their own moral weakness — I am emboldened to propose that before the People of God is described as being without stain or wrinkle, we preface this by a paragraph in which we proclaim to all men, in so many words, that the Church is the household of the Father of mercies in which the failings of prodigal sons are forgiven, their wounds are bound up, their weaknesses are cured, and their needs are answered.[10]

One of the more direct and practical suggestions made about the relationship between the laity and the hierarchy was made by Archbishop Owen McCann of Capetown, South Africa who felt that priests should be given special preparation for dealing with the laity and its apostolate. How important was that observation for today, when there is so much misunderstanding of the role of priest and lay person!

In the Dogmatic Constitution on the Church, the Church is conceived as the People of God whose responsibility it is to preach the gospel to all peoples. This responsibility of the Church was best exemplified in Pope Paul VI's apostolic letter, *Evangelii Nuntiandi*. It is my hope that the Synod of 1987, on the Vocation and Mission of the Laity in the Church and in the World, will further build on that letter and make evangelization the central task of the Church, calling all the faithful to its realization.

After all, the call to all the members of the Church, now addressed as the People of God, is the same. When the Dogmatic Constitution on the Church emphasized participation in the salvific mission of the Church it implied a call, a vocation. It spoke of a universal vocation, a universal call addressed to bishop, priest, religious and lay person alike. It is, therefore, on this theological basis inspired by Vatican II, that the Church's mission is a vocation of the whole Church and not just that of select members. Article 31 of the Constitution puts it this way:

These faithful [the laity] are by baptism made one body with Christ and are established among the People of God. They are in their own way made sharers in the priestly, prophetic, and kingly functions of Christ. They carry out their own part in the mission of the whole Christian people with respect to the Church and the world.

FOOTNOTES

(For full citations of sources, please see the Bibliography)

1. Yzermans, pp. 488-489.
2. Irenaeus, *Against Heresies*, 4:26:2.
3. Yzermans, pp. 477-478.
4. *Council Daybook*, Vol. 3, p. 159.
5. Ibid, p. 138.
6. *Notre Dame Magazine*, Feb., 1985, p. 18.
7. Yzermans, p. 456.
8. Ibid., p. 43.
9. *Council Daybook*, Vol. 1, p. 190.
10. Ibid, p. 38.

VIII.

Ecumenism

The non-Christian world is ever looking at Christians, especially Catholics, and measuring them against the Christian ideal of love of God and neighbor. What must that world think when it compares Catholic behavior with these supernatural ideals? Vatican II went on to meet these ideals head-on and virtually made a public confession of its failures vis-a-vis other Christians and non-Christians in its Decree on Ecumenism, Decree on Eastern Catholic Churches and Declaration on the Relationship of the Church to Non-Christian Religions.

The tragic disunity among Christians is almost as old as Christianity itself. As Xavier Rynne puts it:

> Ignoring the details, it may be said that the sundering of Christendom was effected in three main stages:
>
> 1. First, in the 5th century, the separation of the Nestorian and Monophysite Churches of the East — in Persia (Nestorians or Chaldeans), in Egypt (Copts), and in Syria (Jacobites) — from the Byzantine (Melkite) Church of Rome and Constantinople.
>
> 2. The separation, which became effective in the 11th century, between Rome and Constantinople (involving also all the other Eastern Melkite churches in communion with Constantinople, including the newer churches of Russia, Bulgaria, Serbia, etc.) causing a definite split between Catholics and Orthodox Christians.
>
> 3. In the 16th century, the schism between the Roman Catholic Church and the various Protestant bodies which separated from it. [1]

For the most part these divisions still exist, except for those Oriental Churches or parts of Churches (of the Chaldean, Syrian, Maronite, Coptic, Armenian and Byzantine Rites), that re-established union with the Church of Rome. They are often known as Uniates, but this is not a term they care for. The Ukrainians, for instance, returned to communion with Rome in the latter part of the 16th century.

No subject, therefore, provoked more attention about the Second Vatican Council than its discussion of the Catholic Church's relationship to other religions and its concern for the dignity of the human person. This latter concern embroiled the Council Fathers in heated debate over the subject of religious liberty, which was part of the original schema on ecumenism which came out of the Secretariat for Christian Unity. The subject of religious liberty, which I treat of in Chapter IX, evolved into a separate document of the Council, but its development had profound influence on the Decree on Ecumenism.

After all, Pope John XXIII had Christian unity in mind when he announced an Ecumenical Council for the Church. His *motu proprio* of June 5, 1960, on "Commissions to Prepare for an Ecumenical Council" was most explicit about this:

> By means of this gathering there is quickened once more the hope that those who, though claiming the name of Christian, are yet separated from this Apostolic See, may listen to the voice of the Divine Shepherd and approach the one Church.[2]

Ecumenism in its official form, or the history of its development, was not a familiar subject to many of the Council Fathers. Most bishops could speak on their relationships with other Christians and non-Christians as they faced up to the administration of the sacraments in their dioceses, particularly in the areas of interfaith marriages or participation in worship in other churches. Also, cooperation in civic and other secular programs was not an unfamiliar practice for some bishops.

However, the moment the subject of religious freedom was mentioned in connection with the schema on ecumenism, ears perked up. The bishops from North America began to recall the history of the beginnings of the Catholic Church in their country. The bishops from Eastern Europe were cognizant of the fact that they had to penetrate the Iron Curtain to get to Rome for the Council. Other bishops recalled, with some embarrassment, how the Church in their countries demanded freedom for herself because she was in the minority, while freedom was denied to other Churches in some countries where Catholics were in the majority.

It did not take long before an American, Cardinal Ritter of St. Louis, reminded his fellow bishops that:

> The question of unity among Christians had at its heart the matter of religious freedom. [3]

An interesting exchange took place one morning during our discussion when two prelates from Spain expressed opposite opinions of the wisdom of the schema on ecumenism. One bishop said (and I felt at the time that he was echoing the sentiments of most of his confreres) that the principles of religious freedom should be put at the very beginning of the schema on ecumenism. Another felt that dialogue with Protestants might become a threat to the faith of many Catholics, especially those who were not well educated. The good bishop stressed, in an accent not too easy to grasp, that the schema should include an exhortation to our separated brethren to refrain from proselytism in Catholic countries.

But the confusion and misunderstanding of our discussion on the document on ecumenism was mild until we had to face up to the position of the Jews in the schema. Cardinal Tappouni of Antioch insisted that the inclusion of Jews had no place in a document that was concerned with Christian unity. Cardinal Ruffini went so far as to suggest that the schema should consider those other religions whose members are less hostile to the Catholic Church than the Jews.

Then came the sensational moment on Nov. 18, 1963 when Cardinal Bea, chairman of the commission responsible for the Decree on Ecumenism, rose to announce that he was speaking for Pope John XXIII who desired a separate document on the Jews. The Cardinal later revealed that the Pope had already approved the basic outlines of such a document just a few months before he died. As I indicated earlier, in the interest of unity within the Council itself on this whole matter of religious liberty, the Oriental Churches and the Jews, there were produced in the end three separate documents on each of these subjects.

The ecumenical movement really began among non-Catholics who sought to bring about closer contact with each other — and not only as individual Christians who were interested in unity, but also as denominations or churches who sought common goals. As a matter of historical development, greater effort was made in this regard as a result of the dialogues that began between the Catholic Church and the Protestant Churches after the Council. I served as an observer for the National Conference of Catholic Bishops in several of these dialogues and attended many of the meetings of COCU, the Conference on Christian Union.

Father George Tavard, in writing about the theological setting in this regard prior to Vatican II, states that:

> Most of the theologians of our contemporary renewal have been, at one time or another, in one way or another, involved in the ecumenical movement. There has been a cross-fertilization of Catholic and Protestant thought, not only at the level of biblical scholarship, but also at that of theological reflection. This is indeed a remarkable progress on the attitude of former days, when Protestant theologies were hardly considered to belong among Christian theologies. But this is not simply the result of reading Protestant authors. It is in the first place the logical outcome of the advance of ecclesiological studies in Catholic theology.[4]

A breakthrough for inclusion of the Catholic Church in the ecumenical movement did not occur until the 1950's when an instruction from Rome, *Ecclesia Sancta*, opened the door for dialogue in which Catholic and non-Catholic could meet as equals, "to set forth the teachings of their faith as their own view."[5]

Before that, among Catholics, it was in France and Belgium, at the beginning of this century, that those who were concerned with unity first began to work at it. Dialogue and common interests existed on an unofficial level between Catholics and non-Catholics. As a matter of fact, several Council Fathers referred to this type of relationship in other areas than ecclesiology. There was, for instance, interfaith cooperation in service to the poor during and after World War II. Bishops at the local level strove to meet the problems of mixed marriages by encouraging priests and ministers to work together, and others suggested that the Churches cooperate on solving religious problems touching the public interest.

In that area particularly, Monsignor George Higgins, a peritus at the Council, had this to say when the first draft of the Decree on Ecumenism was being considered:

> I have been in the social action field for 20 years . . . What has been lacking in large part is a sufficient degree of interfaith cooperation in the social order to bring religious principles to bear on the social order . . . There will be more emphasis on a less formal, more flexible lay activity not so directly tied to the directives of the hierarchy.[6]

Indeed, much was done on a cooperative basis by the Catholic Church and her agencies with other Christian and non-Christian groups before Vatican II. During World War II and after, the Catholic bishops of the United States, through their international agency, War Relief Services (later Catholic Relief Services) became involved in worldwide relief and refugee programs. As one of the directors of that agency, I became very much involved with the American Council of Voluntary Agencies, an interdenominational organization that provided effective and coordinated efforts at the national and international levels in bringing food, clothing and medical supplies to the poor, the disadvantaged and displaced people all over the world. Church World Service (a conglomerate of Protestant agencies), Lutheran World Relief, the American Jewish Joint Distribution Committee and Catholic Relief Services were also highly successful in bringing about favorable legislation in the United States for the distribution of surplus food and medical supplies, as well as the immigration of displaced and refugee people to the United States and elsewhere throughout the world.

Archbishop Angelo Roncalli, Apostolic Nuncio to France, who later became Pope John XXIII, personally became involved and was witness to the coordinated efforts of the Church-related agencies involved in European relief and refugee work. As a matter of fact, he attended several of our meetings while Papal Nuncio to France.

With his elevation to the throne of Peter, Pope John realized that more than "material cooperation" was needed at the higher levels of Church government to bring about unity. Providentially then, because of that personal experience of a divided Christianity, he brought new hope to the struggling ecumenical movement with his *motu proprio, Superno Dei Nutu* in June 1960, that authorized the establishment of a Secretariat for Promoting Christian Unity.

In Werner Becker's summary of the words of Cardinal Bea, the first head of that Secretariat:

> According to an early utterance by Cardinal Bea the specific task of the Secretariat during the preparations for the Council was not only to provide information to separated Christians concerning the Council, and to receive their wishes and suggestions, but also to carry out an independent theological review of the themes discussed by the Council, from the ecumenical point of view. The Secretariat shared a responsibility for seeing that the whole Council expressed "the truth, unity and love present in the Catholic Church" in a way which would also be comprehensible to

separated brethren. It was to make known to the Council in an appropriate way the results of its efforts towards a better knowledge of the Church's doctrine and the situation in different countries, as well as of the condition of the ecumenical movement, in a constant awareness that "the Holy Spirit, who is the Spirit of unity, is capable of far more than man."[7]

Noteworthy is the fact that at the fourth general meeting of the Council, on October 22, 1962, Pope John XXIII announced that the Secretariat for Promoting Christian Unity, with all its members and consultors, was now of equal rank to the ten other commissions of the Council. Thus, the work begun by that Secretariat was allowed to come to fruition in the prestigious atmosphere of the Second Vatican Council.

Before I go on to further treatment of the Decree on Ecumenism, it may be important to define our terms. After all, there was some debate in the Council over the use of the words "ecumenical" and "ecumenism." The word "ecumenical" simply means general or universal, or as pertaining to the whole Christian Church. "Ecumenism" is a new word. Interestingly enough, it found its naturalization among English-speaking people as a result of a doctoral thesis, *Catholic Ecumenism*, (Catholic University of America, Washington D.C., 1953). In the Council, the word first appeared in the schema on the Church as Chapter IX *De Oecumenismo* (this chapter does not appear in the final version of the document). It gained popularity and acceptance during the conciliar debates on the subject of Christian unity. In the beginning, however, the German bishops objected to the use of the word "ecumenism." Their unhappiness with the word was based on the ground of a nuance in the German language in which an "ism" has a pejorative meaning. The French-speaking bishops, on the other hand, had become used to the word after the publication of Father Yves Congar's book *Chretiens desunis. Principes d'un oecumenisme catholique*, published as far back as 1937.[8]

In the beginning months of Vatican II, the matter of Christian unity was, as I said, a chapter in the schema on the Church. It suffered the vicissitudes of being lifted out of that famous document (as did several other documents, those on the priesthood, the bishops and the laity), to being one of the sixteen official documents of Vatican II.

The very introduction of the Decree on Ecumenism states that the restoration of Christian unity is one of the principal goals of Vatican II and extols the need for that unity among Christians. It echoes the words of Pope John XXIII, who said that he wanted a Council for the whole Church, that he prayed:

> for a good beginning, continuation, and happy outcome of these proposals for a great work, enlightenment, edification and happiness of all Christian people, for a renewed invitation to the faithful of the separated communities that they also may follow us amiably in this search for unity and grace, to which so many souls aspire in all parts of the earth.[9]

Ten separate Christian denominations were represented at the opening of the Council on October 11, 1962. And, on that day, the Pope in speaking on the "Unity of the Christian Family" again voiced the hope that:

> The Catholic Church, therefore, considers it her duty to work actively so that there may be fulfilled the great mystery of that unity, which Jesus Christ invoked with fervent prayer from His Heavenly Father on the eve of His sacrifice.[10]

As for the reaction of the observers now exposed to all these pleas for unity, they chose a Protestant scholar, Oscar Cullmann, who stated:

> I am not betraying any secrets when I tell you how glad we are to note how a concern for ecumenism pervades these discussions. Yet even here we must be attentive against illusions. We certainly hope with all our hearts that this renewal [of the Catholic Church] will be realized. For we are convinced that, if it is, it will make so much

easier the dialogue between Catholic and non-Catholic that will go on after the council. But we must not forget that these changes will take place inside the Catholic framework and be based on Catholic principles; nor can we object to this to our Catholic brethren, because it would not be good ecumenism to ask them to become Protestant or Orthodox. Still we must face up to reality. Even if the projects for reforms are passed, there will remain important differences between us and Catholicism, even the Catholicism reshaped by this council. However, those who hope for the renewal know this, and that is why the dialogue must go on, and go on under conditions much more favorable, with this renewed Catholicism.[11]

The debates (interventions) on ecumenism in the Council revealed a dichotomy of thought and feeling. But in the end they gave way to what was referred to by scholars as a "convergence of traditions." And no wonder.

It should be remembered that several documents dealing with Christian unity came before the Council Fathers. In reality there were three texts referring to different aspects of an identical problem. The Commission for Eastern (Oriental) Churches had proposed a text on unity titled *De Unitate Ecclesiae: Ut Unum Sint.* In essence the document was concerned exclusively with the principal ways and means of achieving reunion with the Eastern Orthodox. Then the Theological Commission proposed a chapter titled *De Ecumenismo* on Protestants in the schema on the Dogmatic Constitution on the Church. A third proposal, that of the Secretariat for Promoting Christian Unity, was concerned with general ecumenical principles.

Since there were these three proposals so similar in nature, and since the Pope had specifically set up a Secretariat to deal with the problem of Christian unity, a number of bishops asked why that Secretariat had not prepared a single schema, or at least three coordinated drafts, for presentation to the Fathers of the Council.

It was not long before word "leaked out" that the Theological Commission was unwilling to cooperate with any other agency of the Council and desired to monopolize all theological discussion. This was made clear by Bishop De Smedt, speaking for the Secretariat. As Xavier Rynne tells it,

> Msgr. De Smedt then went on to note that, although the Secretariat for Promoting Unity had been created to help with the preparations for the Council and had offered to collaborate with the Theological Commission, "for reasons which I do not care to judge," the Theological Commission "never wished to do so." The Secretariat also proposed the creation of a mixed subcommission, but this offer too was turned down.[12]

In the end, the Council Fathers put things aright. By an almost unanimous vote, they terminated discussion of the various proposals on unity and insisted that the decree prepared by the Secretariat on Christian Unity be accepted as a separate document and that it include the elements of Chapter IX on ecumenism from the schema on the Church. The resolution that brought this action about not only affirmed the true ecumenical purpose of the Council, but expressed the trust the bishops had in the Secretariat for Promoting Christian Unity.

When discussion of the Eastern Churches and the other religions was brought up as part of the schema on ecumenism, so much dissension was provoked that the Coordinating Commission of the Council had to agree to provide for two separate documents covering these subjects.

A document concerning the Catholic Church's relationship to Jews would not have been possible were it not for the personal intervention of Pope John XXIII. The general feeling of the bishops was that the Jews had no place in a document that was concerned with Christian unity. Many bishops were also dissatisfied with the way the Eastern Churches were handled. The final Decree on Eastern Catholic Churches was concerned with those Eastern Churches in communion with Rome, although it also discussed relations with the Eastern Orthodox Churches. The latter, however, were primarily treated in the Decree on Ecumenism.

Again, as in the case of the Constitution on the Sacred Liturgy, the intervention of the Melkite Patriarch Maximos IV Saigh of ancient Antioch, in regard to what later became the Decree on Eastern Catholic Churches, will go down into the history of the Council as a classic:

> The Patriarch declared that the schema under discussion would in fact embitter those of good will among the Orthodox, rather than attract them. The historical outline underlying the document was typically Roman, and concealed the mutual responsibility for the schism of Christianity. In his own words: "The Eastern Churches are apostolic Churches, founded by the apostles. They are not derivative Churches, for they have existed from the very first. The schema does not show how Peter came to have his leading position in the college of bishops. It is necessary to lay more emphasis on the collegiality of the government of the Church, and the papacy would then be manifested as the foundation of this collegiality." The schema is headed "The Unity of the Church" and yet it deals only with our attitude to the Orthodox. As a matter of fact the Orthodox are much closer to us Catholics than are the Protestants. The only question which still divides us is that of the Roman primacy. "For us Eastern Catholics this separation from our Eastern brethren is a fearful torment, which strikes our inmost heart. Reunion is our greatest desire, and we are prepared for the utmost sacrifice to achieve it. They and we are *one* family, and consequently we desire to forget the dissension of the past and human considerations, and to unite ourselves with them in Christ, in order to realize his prayer: 'That they may be one.' "[13]

Many of us bishops from the West, although familiar with the subject from our earlier studies of Church history, gained new insights on how deep were the divisions between the Christians of the East and the West. Some notes I have, apparently written after a stop at one of the coffee bars in St. Peter's, and following on the magnificent intervention of Patriarch Maximos, make reference to a bishop who wisely observed that the ''elements which unite the Catholic Church with the Oriental Churches are greater than those which divide them.'' Even here, though, ''Catholic Church'' would seem to be unconsciously identified with ''Western, Latin Rite Church.'' And this sort of casual identification is of great concern to the Eastern Churches.

But bitterness prevailed, perhaps because the Orientals came to the Council with some well-founded suspicions. They found it difficult, for instance, to set aside thought of the approach of Pope Leo XIII whose undue insistence on unity with the Church of the West would deny the dignity, rights and obligations of Eastern Christians and the traditions they held to so firmly over the centuries. Cardinal Leger of Montreal, Canada surfaced the problem when he said that:

> Because of undue insistence on unity in the past, the false impression is given that the Church promotes a monolithic unity which entails excessive uniformity in doctrine, liturgy and so on. In our insistence on unity, we have too often lost sight of the advantages of diversity.
>
> Charity and truth must not suffer in our discussions. But we must pursue truth in humility as well as in charity. Since separation became a sad reality, our separated brethren have been engaged in their own doctrinal research. Discrepancies between them and us cannot be resolved without joint theological investigation.
>
> The Church has known many heresies and schisms. The remedy is not necessarily authority, but humble progress in the Faith.[14]

A number of other prelates followed in the spirit of Cardinal Leger's intervention. Cardinal Ritter of St. Louis, Missouri, felt that ''we should present unity not merely as a goal of inestimable value, but in such a way as to show disunion as an evil of equal magnitude.'' The Auxiliary Bishop of Rome, Giovanni Canestri reacted with: ''Our separated brethren have a right to know what kind of unity we are inviting them to.'' And George Dwyer, Bishop of Leeds, England, stated that: "We should not be deluded into thinking that a few kind words and a spirit of cordiality will bring on union in the immediate future."[15]

As I indicated earlier, Pope John XXIII personally intervened in the preparation of a statement on the relationship between the Church and the people of Israel. It was known that various appeals had reached the Pope from Jewish leaders for information on the Council. The Pope referred the requests of the Jewish community to his Secretariat for Unity. When discussion of the Church's relationship to the Jews was brought to the floor of St. Peter's, Cardinal Bea, the head of that Secretariat, was in a good position to advise and direct us. He told us that various approaches were made by the Jewish side in preparation for the Decree on Ecumenism. A commentary on the Declaration on the Relationship of the Church to Non-Christian Religions (in which the statement on the Jews appeared) provides this information on Jewish influence on the Council:

Cardinal Bea's reference to various applications from the Jewish side doubtless included that of the French historian, Jules Isaac, the most important advocate, before the Council began, of Jewish concerns. In the early summer of 1960 he went to Rome, to make his wishes known to Pope John, with the support of the French branch of B'nai B'rith and equipped with a letter of introduction from Mgr. de Provencères, Archbishop of Aix-en-Provence, where he lived. After initial difficulties he succeeded in obtaining an audience on 13 June of the same year, with the help of the French Ambassador to the Holy See, M. de la Tournelle, and of the present Under-Secretary of the Secretariat for Unity, Mgr. G. Arrighi. The Pope began the conversation, with his characteristic ease of manner, by speaking of his great reverence for the Old Testament, especially for the prophets, the psalms, and the book of Wisdom. Isaac, on the other hand, was a man who believed he did not have much more time: he went straight to the point. He referred to the great hope that the measures taken by the Pope concerning the Jews had awakened in the hearts of the people of the old dispensation.

"If we expect still more," he added, "what is responsible for that, if not the great 'goodness of the Pope'?" During the audience he gave the Pope a dossier in three parts: 1. A brief for the correction of false and indeed unjust statements about Israel in Christian teaching. 2. As an example, the theological myth that the scattering of Israel was a punishment inflicted by God on the people for the crucifixion of Jesus. 3. An extract from the catechism of Trent which in its treatment of the Passion emphasized the guilt of all sinners as the fundamental cause of Christ's death upon the cross, and thus, in Isaac's view, proved that the accusation of deicide raised against the Jews did not belong to the true tradition of the Church.[16]

It is questionable whether Jules Isaac influenced the Pope to the extent many felt he did. Certainly, he met with the Pope at a time when preparation for the Council began to take shape. No doubt, the Pope also was thinking about the relationship between the Church and the Jews, especially since he had already established the Secretariat for Unity. Then too, the Pope had already taken measures, before meeting with Isaac, to remove certain phrases from liturgical texts that were offensive to the Jews. The change in the Good Friday prayer a year before, when the reference to "the perfidious Jews" was omitted, is a good example.

In the fall of 1960, while attending a meeting at the headquarters of Catholic Relief Services in New York, I had occasion to meet an old friend, the head of the American Jewish Joint Distribution Committee, a foreign relief agency. My friend told me that he would accompany a representative group of his parent agency, the United Jewish Appeal, to Europe and the Middle East on a fact-finding tour and that they hoped for an audience with the Pope. A post card from Rome advised me that, indeed, they were granted an audience with Pope John XXIII, and that he had greeted them with the words: "I am Joseph, your brother!" How typical of the Pope, I thought, to have drawn this phrase from the Old Testament to make his visitors at ease.

Later, when I was invited to participate in the proceedings of the Second Vatican Council, I learned that the Pope had used that phrase before, in his first encyclical, *Ad Petri Cathedram*, when on June 29, 1959, he announced his intention to call a Council.

Given the Pope's diplomatic experience, there was no doubting his eagerness to heal the rift that existed between Christians and Jews. In France, where he was the Apostolic Nuncio, those of us who worked for Catholic Relief Services shared not only his table, but brought back to him information about our visits to Germany and the horrifying atrocities that had occurred there during the Second World War.

Unfortunately, Pope John did not live to witness fruition of his efforts to heal the rift between Christians and Jews. His final words at the closing of the first session of the Council appear to be a portent of his death:

> In this hour of heartfelt joy it is as if the heavens were opened above our heads and the splendor of the heavenly court shines out upon us, filling us with superhuman certainty and a supernatural spirit of faith, joy and profound peace. [17]

Pope Paul VI, who succeeded Pope John, lost no time in stressing his determination to follow through on the goals his predecessor had set for the Council. In a letter to the Dean of the Sacred College of Cardinals, Eugene Tisserant, advising him of the opening of the second session on September 29, 1963, he stressed "the encouragement and hastening of the unity between separated brothers and the Catholic Church." His personal invitation to the bishops to return to Rome again emphasized "the Church's solicitude to favor union among men, in the first place among those who profess themselves to be Christian." And in his opening address on that September day he assured non-Catholics that the door of the Church is open to them.

The electrifying address therefore, of Cardinal Bea to the Council on November 19, 1963 in which he was given the opportunity to expound the fourth chapter of the schema on ecumenism, "The Declaration on the Christian Attitude toward Jews," had my rapt attention. But I was not alone. Other eyes and ears were fixed on this German-born Jesuit priest and Prince of the Church who apparently had not only deep feelings about the atrocities suffered by the Jewish people in his homeland, but was caught up with Pope John's determination to eliminate hostility toward Jews. Needless to say, the standing ovation that greeted the humble Cardinal when he finished gave new meaning to the words we bishops sang again and again during the Council sessions: "Ubi caritas et amor, Deus ibi est" (Where charity and love prevail, there is God).

Approximately ten days prior to Cardinal Bea's moving speech to the Council Fathers, we were given the draft of a statement on Anti-Semitism which might be communicated to the world. That statement and the inclusion of a declaration on Jewish/Christian relations into the schema on ecumenism provoked, needless to say, bitter debate.

The reaction of prelates from the Arab world was, to say the least, most unfriendly. Cardinal Tappouni, the Syrian Rite Patriarch of Antioch, led off the opposition by stating that neither the Jews nor the subject of religious liberty should be treated in the schema on ecumenism. He also felt that:

> The present-day political situation is such that this text [on Christian/Jewish relations] is likely to engender confusion.[18]

Bishop Michael Rodrigues of India put that notion another way when he said:

> No matter what precautions we take, it is inevitable that this council text will be misinterpreted for political reasons. It will cause trouble in Arab nations and in Asiatic countries which have very ancient religions not mentioned in the schema.[19]

The Coptic Rite Patriarch Stephanos I Sidarouss of Alexandria, Egypt, was firm in stating that:

"A whole chapter devoted to the Jews is completely out of place in a discussion of Christian unity." For the rest, he declared that a statement on Anti-Semitism was unnecessary since the Church has already indicated its position on that score. [20]

The Melkite Patriarch of Antioch, Maximos IV Saigh, took another tack:

Ecumenism is a striving for the reunion of the entire Christian family, that is to say, the rejoining of all who are baptized in Christ. It is, then, a family matter, strictly intimate. If so, non-Christians do not enter into the matter. And we do not see what the Jews are doing in Christian ecumenism, and why they have been introduced into it. Besides, it is seriously offensive to our separated brethren that they should seem to be treated on the same footing with the Jews. [21]

It can be assumed — given the Pope's keen interest in some form of treatment of the "Jewish question," and Cardinal Bea's support of his position—that the latter's address I referred to above was a strategically arranged move to bring some balance to the discussions on ecumenism.

However, fate intervened. Pope Paul VI announced his intention of making a pilgrimage to the Holy Land. It was a brilliant move, and further discussion of the schema on ecumenism ceased in order to eliminate any embarrassment for the Pope. The pilgrimage was a huge success. On entering Israeli territory the Pope, in responding to a greeting by the President of the State of Israel, responded:

As a pilgrim of peace we beg above all for the blessing of reconciliation of men with God and of deep and genuine concord among men and peoples.

And then again, as he worshipped in the Church of the Holy Sepulchre he took up this theme, in a form of confession:

> Lord Jesus, we have come here as guilty men to the place of our crime. We have come like the one who followed thee and yet betrayed thee. We have so often been both true and false. [22]

On September 25, 1964, near the beginning of the third session of the Council, Cardinal Bea solemnly introduced the Declaration on the Jews and Non-Christians. He emphasized that no other document had so held the public in suspense and been so much written about. He felt so deeply about the document that he ventured to say that people would judge the Council by the way the bishops handled this question of the Jews.

The first to support the Cardinal's position and the Declaration itself were the German bishops who, through a spokesman of their Conference stated:

> We German bishops welcome the Council Decree on the Jews. If the Church in the Council makes a statement concerning her own nature, she cannot fail to mention her connection with God's people of the Old Covenant. We are convinced that this Council Declaration provides an opportunity for renewed contact and a better relationship between the Church and the Jewish people. [23]

Cardinal Ritter of St. Louis quickly followed with this decisive statement:

> With all my heart I gladly make this Declaration my own. Quite clearly, it meets a need of our time. I speak of a need, not of some political or national pressure to be evaded or appeased, nor of some human approval to be sought for, but quite simply of a centuries-old injustice that cries aloud for reparation. For many centuries we Christians have been guilty of error and injustice towards the Jews. In many ways we have assumed that God . . . had abandoned this people. Christians, and even ecclesiastical documents, have charged the Jewish people with the suffering and death of Christ. In prayer they were called the "perfidious," the "deicidal" people,

who ''once called down upon themselves the blood of the Savior.'' We who are gathered here in this Ecumenical Council have today been given an opportunity to root out such errors and injustices and to make reparation (for the injuries these have caused).[24]

Joining Cardinal Ritter were his confreres. Cardinal Cushing of Boston spoke of our common heritage with the Jews:

But surely we ought to indicate the fact that we sons of Abraham according to the spirit must show a special esteem and particular love for the sons of Abraham according to the flesh because of this common patrimony. As sons of Adam, they are our brothers: As sons of Abraham, they are the blood brothers of Christ.[25]

Cardinal Meyer of Chicago presented the lengthiest intervention and in it pointed out:

Is it not true, on this point, that our task is rather to set forth the whole truth about the Jews, more or less according to the mind of St. Thomas (ST III, q.47, art. 5, *in corpus*), as was done in the earlier text? For St. Thomas, on the basis of Sacred Scripture, laid down these two points: 1) None of the Jews of the time of Christ was formally and subjectively guilty of deicide since all were ignorant of Christ's divinity. This ought to be said explicitly in our text. 2) The mass of the Jews must be absolved of all formal guilt because they followed the leaders out of ignorance. In proof of this, St. Thomas advances the words of St. Peter: ''I know that you did this out of ignorance, as did your leaders'' (Ac 3:17).

Finally, something will have to be stated about where the true cause of the sufferings of Christ is to be sought: ''He died for us and for our salvation!''[26]

After going through four drafts, the Declaration on the Jews became the center of the final Declaration on the Relationship of the Church to Non-Christian Religions. This final document came to a vote just the day before the third session of the Council was to end, but only after Cardinal Bea made this final plea:

> It is impossible to draw up a Declaration which would not, in any passage, be open to misinterpretation by one side and at the same time satisfy the other side. Besides, it must be borne in mind that it is more important to have such a solemn Declaration by the Council than to satisfy everyone, even if that were possible.[27]

As Father Walter Abbott, the compiler of the Vatican II documents, observed:

> Many sentences and sections of Vatican II decrees are remarkable for the fact that they are there at all. It can truly be said that the whole Decree on Ecumenism is remarkable for that fact. In this Decree, the focus is more on a "pilgrim" Church moving toward Christ than on a movement of "return" to the Roman Catholic Church. In this Decree, the Council goes beyond the assertion that the Catholic Church is the true Church to assert that Jesus, in His Spirit, is at work in the Churches and Communities beyond the visible borders of the Catholic Church; the Council asserts that believers in Christ who are baptized are truly reborn and truly our brothers and that God uses their worship to sanctify and save them . . .
>
> It has been said that the Decree on Ecumenism is not an end but a new beginning full of hopes and promises. The Constitution on the Sacred Liturgy marked the arrival of the vernacular movement, but it was a beginning rather than an end. The Constitution on Divine Revelation marked the establishment of the kerygmatic movement — again a beginning rather than an end of a movement. The Decree on Ecumenism marks the full entry of the Roman Catholic Church into the ecumenical movement. It is evident that much has been accomplished by the Decree, but what counts more is what remains to be done.[28]

FOOTNOTES

(For full citations of sources, please see the Bibliography)

1. Rynne, p. 189.
2. *Council Daybook*, Vol. 1, p. 4.
3. Ibid., p. 271.
4. Tavard, p. 37.
5. AAS, No. 42, pp. 142-147.
6. *Council Daybook*, Vol. 1, p. 108.
7. *Commentary*, Vol. 2, pp. 2-3.
8. Ibid., pp. 57-58.
9. *Council Daybook*, Vol. 1, p. 2.
10. Ibid., p. 28.
11. Ibid., p. 91.
12. Rynne, pp. 162-163.
13. *Commentary*, Vol. 2, p. 11.
14. *Council Daybook*, Vol. 1, pp. 301-302.
15. Ibid., pp. 302, 310.
16. *Commentary*, Vol. 3, p. 2.
17. *Council Daybook*, Vol. 1, p. 121.
18. Ibid., p. 271.
19. Ibid., p. 293.
20. Ibid., p. 272.
21. Ibid.
22. *Commentary*, Vol. 3, p. 57.
23. Ibid., p. 68.
24. Ibid.
25. *Council Daybook*, Vol. 2, p. 71; Yzermans, p. 586.
26. Yzermans, p. 589.
27. *Commentary*, Vol. 3, p. 99.
28. Abbott, pp. 338-339.

IX.

The Theology Of Liberty

In the questionnaires returned by the world's bishops prior to the Council, the demand for some discussion of the issue of Church-State relations was almost universal, given especially the problem of the spread of Communism. It is interesting to note that the Iron and Bamboo Curtains kept 111 bishops from attending the sessions of Vatican II. However, out of a total of 70 Polish bishops, 27 were able to attend the Council. All of the 28 Yugoslav bishops were allowed to attend. Seven bishops came from East Germany; 19 exiled Ukrainian bishops came to the Council; none from the Soviet Union, Bulgaria or Hungary came; and only 3 out of the 15 Czechoslovak bishops attended. None of the bishops from the Communist countries of the Far East came, since most of them were in jail at the time of the Council.

Pope Paul VI referred to the absence of the bishops from the Communist countries in several of his talks. In a homily at the public meeting of the Council on October 28, 1965 at which he promulgated the Declaration on Religious Freedom, he said:

> We are happy to have around us concelebrating at this apostolic altar bishops who are dear to us and who represent countries where liberty — to which the Gospel has a supreme right—is restricted if not refused, and where some of them are witnesses of the sufferings which Christ foretold to His apostles. To these bishops, to the

Churches whose suffering they bring to mind, to the countries which their presence makes us love all the more, we send an expression of our solidarity, our love, and our prayers for better days.[1]

As Jesuit Father John Courtney Murray, the principal architect of the Declaration on Religious Freedom, envisioned it:

For twenty centuries the Church has been looking in on herself, but if and when this issue of religious liberty does come up, as it must, there will be need of the Church's experience of this issue in America and of the wisdom that has been at the root of this experience as it must now be applied to the countries who are denied religious freedom.[2]

For Father Murray the issue of religious liberty was, of course, of the highest interest to him as a theologian and as an American. It was, in his opinion, the American issue at the Second Vatican Council.

Respect for individual differences and preferences was a dominating factor in the Council proceedings. In the very last session of the Council, the bishops stressed in an official document the value and dignity of the human person. The first paragraph of the Declaration on Religious Freedom begins:

A sense of the dignity of the human person has been impressing itself more and more deeply on the consciousness of contemporary man. And the demand is increasingly made that men should act on their own judgment, enjoying and making use of a responsible freedom, not driven by coercion but motivated by a sense of duty (#1).

Despite much heated controversy on the Council floor of St. Peter's, this document marked a turning point in the history of the Church.

The Council Fathers also stressed human dignity when in the Pastoral Constitution on the Church they said:

Hence man's dignity demands that he act according to a knowing and free choice. Such a choice is personally motivated and prompted from within. It does not result from either blind internal impulse nor from mere external pressure. Man achieves such dignity when, emancipating himself from all captivity to passion, he pursues his goal in a spontaneous choice of what is good, and procures for himself, through effective and skillful action, apt means to that end. Since man's freedom has been damaged by sin, only by God's grace can he bring such a relationship with God into full flower (#17).

Just what was at the base of the problem that gave rise to some of the controversy at the Council on the schema on religious freedom? It was simply this: the adaptation of the Church to a world in which she could no longer impose her own authority with force. For example, where Catholics were in the minority, they would have to appeal to liberty of conscience; where they were in the majority, they would have to respect the sincere convictions and the liberty of conscience of others. But there was more to this ethic of behavior. The Church herself needed to react to the historical perspective of the burden that:

has to be borne by the individual conscience, since for too long it had been charged with taking away its member's freedom by making virtue consist essentially in observance of a code of law rather than in faithfulness to all the promptings of the Holy Spirit wherever that Spirit may lead.[3]

Then again, the Declaration on Religious Freedom, one of the highlights of Vatican II, was controversial largely because it brought to the surface with extraordinary vigor the theological issue that lay continually below the surface of all the conciliar debates — the issue of the development of doctrine. Father Murray, in his introduction to the Declaration on Religious Freedom, felt that:

The notion of development, not the notion of religious freedom, was the real sticking-point for many of those who opposed the Declaration even to the end. The course of the development between the *Syllabus of Errors* (1864), and *Dignitatis Humanae Personae* [The Declaration on Religious Freedom] (1965) still remains to be explained by theologians. But the Council formally sanctioned the validity of the development itself; and this was a doctrinal event of high importance for theological thought in many other areas.[4]

There you have the reason why I chose to title this chapter, "The Theology of Liberty." Another reason was that the acclaim in the media that followed the promulgation of the Declaration on Religious Freedom did not reflect the document's theological content, but rather its political implications.

And finally, for the same reasons, the reader will want to reflect on Bishop De Smedt's reasons (quoted below; cf. fn. 5) why the subject of religious freedom had to be considered by the Council.

Error, according to those bishops who were opposed to the document, did not enjoy the same rights as truth. This view reflected the thinking of the Theological Commission that only the person who is in possession of the truth has the right to religious freedom. The implication, as will be noted later in this chapter, was that only the Catholic religion was in possession of the truth. How this belief, on the part of those of us bishops who supported religious freedom, could be maintained in the light of the discussions we were engaged in on ecumenism, was difficult to understand.

And further, it should be remembered that prior to the Council, the "old philosophy," essentialism (or Thomism, after St. Thomas Aquinas), had a profound influence on the Church. That teaching and belief was concerned more with the objective side of the human person than with the subjective side. The subjective side of our human nature was often considered to be the "lower side," that of emotion and feeling. Thus, the opponents of the schema on religious freedom were concerned more with the objective state of people's beliefs (that is, whether they held to the true faith or not) rather than their subjective state (that is, whether they did so in good faith).

The debate on the religious freedom schema came late on the Council's agenda. Toward the end of the third session it was almost discarded, but by that time the bishops already exhibited a readiness to enter into dialogue among themselves and with the world — so much so, that the final document was overwhelmingly approved by the bishops.

Actually, there were six different schemata presented to the Council Fathers on the subject of religious freedom. The first text was part of chapter 5 of the schema on ecumenism, a work of the Secretariat for Promoting Christian Unity. Before that, religious freedom had been a matter for consideration as part of the Pastoral Constitution on the Church.

The first text was composed before Pope John XXIII had published his encyclical *Pacem in Terris*, yet it reflected an identical doctrine — namely, that Christians ought to maintain and exhibit toward their separated brethren a correct attitude with regard to the necessary freedom of the act of faith. The second text became the lengthy "relatio," or introduction to chapter 5 of the ecumenism schema by Bishop Emile De Smedt of Bruges, a member of the Secretariat for Promoting Christian Unity. It was put before the Council on November 19, 1963. The date is important in that the debacle that threatened the very life of the schema on religious freedom occurred on the same date one year later.

Bishop De Smedt's speech was one of the high points of the second session of the Council. It was remarkable for its clarity, sincerity and conviction. It was greeted with prolonged applause and thus reflected the thinking of the Council Fathers. The Belgian bishop began by giving four reasons why the Council, in response to numerous requests, must consider the subject:

Very many Conciliar Fathers have insistently demanded that this Sacred Synod clearly explain and proclaim the right of man to religious liberty. Among the reasons given, four principal ones should be listed:

1) Truth: The Church must teach and defend the right to religious liberty because there is question of the truth, the care of which was committed to her by Christ;

2) Defense: The Church cannot remain silent today when almost half of mankind is deprived of religious liberty by atheistic materialism of various kinds;

3) Peaceful Social Life: Today in all nations of the world, men, who adhere to different religions or who lack all religious belief, must live together in one and the same human society; in the light of truth, the Church should point the way toward living together peacefully;

4) Ecumenism: Many non-Catholics harbor an aversion against the Church or at least suspect her of a kind of Machiavellianism because we seem to them to demand the free exercise of religion when Catholics are in a minority in any nation and at the same time refuse and deny the same religious liberty when Catholics are in the majority. [5]

Here, Bishop De Smedt emphasized the two principal points of Pope John's encyclical *Pacem in Terris* upon which his very effective talk was based:

On the question of religious liberty, the principal document is the encyclical *Pacem in Terris*, in which Pope John XXIII especially developed these two points of doctrine: 1) by the law of nature, the human person has the right to the free exercise of religion in society according to the dictates of a sincere conscience (*conscientia recta*), whether the conscience be true (*conscientia vera*), or the captive either of error or of inadequate knowledge of truth and of sacred things. 2) To this right corresponds the duty incumbent upon other men and the public authority to recognize and respect that right in such a way that the human person in society is kept immune from all coercion of any kind (cf. AAS 55, 1963, p. 299; p. 264 and pp. 273-274). [6]

It is interesting that Bishop De Smedt stressed the fact that the chapter on religious liberty was not a dogmatic treatise but a pastoral approach intended for people of today. Yet he was hinting (like Father Murray) that the theology needed to be worked out by others.

When decisive voting began on the different elements of the ecumenism schema in November, 1963, religious liberty took over the limelight—despite the best efforts of the moderators to have the bishops give their attention to the subject of Christian unity. And so it was, that in order not to lose sight of one of the main concerns of the Council, unity among Christians, the bishops were told that at a later date a vote would be taken separately on the crucial fifth chapter of the schema, treating religious liberty. The tremendous applause that greeted that announcement gave clear indication to the opposition that the subject of religious liberty could not be scuttled. However, the next session of the Council showed how strong, persistent and influential the opposition was.

There had been, of course, ample opportunity for the Council Fathers to examine, between sessions, what was now the second schema on religious liberty. More than 280 pages of emendations were sent in by mail to the Secretariat for Promoting Christian Unity, which was still handling the schema. Many bishops expressed the conviction that the subject of religious liberty merited separate consideration, apart from being just a chapter of the ecumenism schema. They wanted the Council to produce a special document on religious freedom.

> The reason given for it was that religious freedom was a subject transcending in importance and extent the limits of ecumenism; for it was absolutely essential also for the relations of the Church to all mankind.[7]

The Coordinating Committee of the Council shared this view and, on April 18, 1964, ruled that religious liberty be presented to the Council at its next session as a separate declaration. And with that, it commissioned the Secretariat for Promoting Christian Unity to prepare a third version.

When, however, the Council reconvened for its third session the indomitable opposition came up with a new reason for eliminating consideration of a schema on religious freedom. It questioned the competency of the Secretariat for Promoting Christian Unity to improve the schema. Despite the subtlety of the opposition, the Council President announced that the Coordinating Committee had decided in favor of the Secretariat. Again, the applause that reverberated on St. Peter's walls gave clear indication of where the majority of the bishops stood on the matter of religious liberty.

That joy was short-lived. Consideration of the third schema was mysteriously shelved. The official report given to the bishops simply stated that "an important group of bishops" demanded that, according to article 30, paragraph 2 of the "Ordinamento" (rules that governed the Council proceedings), the discussion and voting on a third schema on religious liberty should be delayed, so that there would be sufficient time for a thorough examination of the new text. The "behind the scenes" machinations of the opposition worked this time to the consternation of the bishops.

The sequence of events went like this: On November 17, 1964, the third schema on religious liberty was presented to the bishops for discussion. On that same day, the Secretary General announced that a vote on the new version would take place on November 19. But on that day (now labeled in the history of the Council as "Black Thursday") Cardinal Tisserant, Dean of the Council presidency rose, stopped the proceedings, and announced that the Council Presidents, in conformity with the rules, decided not to proceed to a vote on the document on religious liberty as was announced.

There was a hush in St. Peter's. We turned to each other in wonderment and tried to determine what was going on up front at the Presidents' table. From a distance I noticed that my Archbishop, Cardinal Meyer of Chicago, rose from his chair, turned to his colleagues nearby, and moments later approached Cardinal Tisserant who had just made that startling announcement.

Many of the bishops began to leave their places to gather in small groups in an effort to assess the meaning of the announcement and its effect on the future of the schema on religious liberty. I rushed behind the tier of stalls to the front of the aula. I reached the Cardinal's chair but stood back in deference to His Eminence who was obviously agitated and in lively conversation with several other prelates. A few moments later I noticed Father John Courtney Murray nearby and Cardinal Meyer inviting him to join that circle of disturbed prelates.

Xavier Rynne describes the scene this way:

> When Cardinal Meyer and the other presidents and moderators left their places and pandemonium broke loose on the council floor, the Pope, who was watching the scene on his closed circuit TV, telephoned Archbishop Felici and ordered him to come to his apartment at once. With the forceful, restraining figure of the domineering Secretary General gone from the hall, the pent-up emotions of the bishops were given free play. Muttering "This man is hopeless," Cardinal Meyer stalked away from Tisserant and joined a group of prelates and *periti* [among them Father Murray] gathering beside the tribune on the left side of the nave.[8]

On the way home for lunch at the Chicago House of Studies on Via Sardegna, our normally calm and dignified Cardinal was disturbed and in no mood to talk. Bishop O'Donnell, Msgr. Bergin (the Cardinal's secretary) and I shared that silence with the hope that we would learn what really happened up there at the Presidents' Table.

Later that evening at dinner, we learned from Cardinal Meyer that the postponement of the vote had not been discussed with the members of the Presidency of the Council and that this was why he got up from his chair and went around to the front of the table to argue and remonstrate with Cardinal Tisserant. The only reply he got was that the decision had been made and there would be no change.

What really shocked him was that those who had manipulated the decision announced by Cardinal Tisserant had so quickly forgotten the prophetic words of Pope Paul VI at the opening of the second session of the Council. He went to his study and brought back to the table the text of the Pope's speech which said:

> What displeasure to see that in certain countries religious liberty, like other fundamental rights of man, is being crushed by principles and methods of political, racial or anti-religious intolerance! The heart grieves to have to observe that in the world there are still so many acts of injustice against goodness and the free profession of one's religious faith.[9]

The next morning, at the last meeting of the third session of the Council, Cardinal Tisserant read a note from Pope Paul VI, advising the bishops that the question of religious liberty would be the very first matter for discussion and vote at the next session of the Council. Repeated applause greeted this announcement.

Thus, this exciting affair ended without the Council having been able to vote on the third schema on religious liberty. Cardinal Tisserant did remind the Fathers, however, that they could still submit their views on that schema in writing to the General Secretariat up until February 17, 1965.

The bustle of departures, the sounds of leave-taking as the third session ended were followed by an oppressive emptiness, similar to what the bishops experienced at the close of the first session in 1962.

In three years the bishops had given the Catholic Church just five of the sixteen documents that were the product of Vatican II. The bishops wondered if they would ever catch up, or whether the Council would go on for several more years. Those last weeks of the third session were full of anxieties because of what was happening to the subject of religious liberty. The atmosphere was strained and many bishops were glad they were going home.

But the basic reason for those anxieties was the lack of information about what was happening behind the scenes. Bishop Ernest Primeau of New Hampshire, one of my classmates, and a long-time resident of Rome, called it "Romanita" (the Roman way of doing things). As we walked out the front doors of St. Peter's after the closing Mass of the third session of the Council, he gestured to the left and said, as I remember his words: "Within those walls that surround the Vatican one just does not know what man or what office is responsible for certain decisions. One never learns what procedures are used to arrive at a decision."

Between the closing of the third session of the Council on November 21, 1964, and the opening of the fourth and last session on September 14, 1965, the fourth schema on religious liberty was developed. More than 218 suggestions for improvement of the text had been mailed in to the Secretariat for Promoting Christian Unity. During February, 1965, a group of theologians and advisers examined the individual suggestions very carefully and then began the work of preparing proposals for a new schema. By early spring, the Theological Commission had sent in its own suggestions. In May of that year the Coordinating Commission approved the new schema and Pope Paul VI authorized its mailing to the Council Fathers. It was a document of some 54 pages that would form the basis for further discussion on the subject of religious liberty when the bishops returned to Rome for the last session of the Council.

In keeping with the promise he had made the year before, when Cardinal Tisserant opened the fourth session of the Second Vatican Council on September 20, 1965, the very first item for discussion was the new, or fourth schema on religious liberty. Sixty-two oral interventions were made. The Secretariat for Promoting Christian Unity then made a plea to the Council authorities that they seek a definitive decision from the Council Fathers, since a vote had yet to be had from them on the matter of religious liberty. The Coordinating Committee of the Council met that evening and decided that there was to be no vote. The Pope, however, intervened and decided the next day that the bishops were to make known their feelings that very same morning. 1997 bishops voted in favor of the fourth schema on religious liberty and 224 against.

Just what was the nature of some of the interventions that characterized discussion of the schema on religious freedom? Here, we are backtracking in time to the third session of the Council in 1964. It should be remembered that the subject of religious liberty at this time was still a part of the document on ecumenism and the responsibility of the Secretariat for Promoting Christian Unity. That is why Cardinal Ritter of St. Louis expressed satisfaction that the schema on ecumenism contained a chapter on religious freedom. He felt that without such a statement by the Council, there was no chance for a real dialogue between Catholics and those of other faiths. He even urged that the schema be cleared of expressions that might be offensive to Protestants.

Cardinal Meyer of Chicago, speaking on behalf of the American hierarchy in 1964, had emphasized that the decree was in accord with Pope John's teaching in the encyclical *Pacem in Terris*. He insisted that with certain textual changes, the decree would clarify and advance the traditional teaching of the Church on this subject. He added that its passage was absolutely necessary for these five reasons:

> First, men want from the Church the promotion of religious liberty. Second, because it will give the Church the opportunity of giving example to governments as to how they should treat religious bodies within their borders. Third, it will teach Catholics that true religion consists in the free, generous and conscious acceptance of God. Fourth, the apostolate of the Church will be assisted by the demonstration that none can be led to the Faith by force but only by hearing, preaching and receiving the gift of God. Finally, it will lead to a fruitful dialogue with non-Catholics and work for the cause of Christian unity. [10]

Then the Cardinal went on most strongly to state that if the declaration were not passed, nothing else enacted by the Council would make much difference.

One of the more brilliant presentations was made by Bishop John Wright of Pittsburgh, who spoke on the question of religious liberty and its exercise vis-a-vis the State:

> All sides agree that the question of religious liberty and its exercise ultimately touches the question of the common good. Therefore, the analysis and defense of religious liberty ought to take into account the nature and protection of that common good which, in a way, constitutes the very *res publica* and thus must be promoted by the directors of the State.[11]

Archbishop Karl Alter, President of the American Bishops' Conference, and the first to request that the subject of religious liberty be discussed in the Council, speaking on behalf of many of the bishops of the United States said:

> We, however, wish to append certain observations. First, we are not speaking of any kind of liberty or of undetermined religious liberty, or of liberty understood in the wider sense. We are speaking precisely of that right of a human person to immunity from all external force in religious matters, whether induced by civil power or any other power. In the second session of the Council, the very excellent Relator brought to light this distinction between true religious liberty and all other false types. The right of a person to teach errors or perpetuate evil has never been affirmed in any way. . . Secondly, it seems especially desirable to us and, even more so, necessary for promoting peace and harmony in civil society that this question should be treated in clear and unambiguous language in this schema on ecumenism of the Second Vatican Council.[12]

On the negative side, or at least in an attempt to water down the schema on religious freedom, Cardinal Ernesto Ruffini of Palermo reflected much of the thinking of the Italian hierarchy. He proposed that the title of the schema be changed to read, "Freedom to Profess Religion" or "Free Exercise of Religion."

> He warned against confusing freedom with tolerance. Freedom is proper to truth, he said, and only truth has rights. Tolerance must be patient and kindly, he said.[13]

A Spanish prelate, Fernando Cardinal Quiroga y Palacios of Santiago de Compostella, called for a complete revision of the declaration on the grounds that while it furthered union with separated Christians, it ignored grave dangers to the faith and charity of Catholics. He felt that it had been written for Protestant countries with no thought to the situation in Catholic countries.[14]

Cardinal Ottaviani, head of the Holy Office in Rome, took exception to the statement that man, even in error, is worthy of honor.

> Cardinal Ottaviani said the declaration contains elements beyond ecumenism and does not pay sufficient attention to non-Christian religions. He declared that attention must be paid not only to natural rights but also to supernatural rights, and added that those professing a revealed religion have rights over and above those coming from natural law.[15]

Returning to the fourth session of the Council in 1965: after the discussion on the fourth schema had been completed, the Secretariat for Promoting Christian Unity moved to the composition of a fifth text which was completed in just one month. That fifth schema had 86 pages and contained fifteen articles. It differed from the fourth in its concern for the basis of religious freedom and the duties of public authorities with regard to it. The schema especially emphasized the dignity of the human person in its relation to truth. It stressed that public authority has the duty to assure that the members of society have sufficient possibilities to exercise their rights and to fulfill their religious duties.

Despite the fact that the Council Fathers voted in favor of the fifth schema on October 26, 1965 with "yes" and "no" votes, a second method of voting on Council documents (that is, "jutta modum," which means that although the voter agreed to the substance of the document, he also was asking for a change according to a "manner" suggested by him) provoked so many "modi" or changes (almost 600 of them), that a special working group was formed to consider the more important suggestions. That working group of theologians and advisers, after studying all the modi, had to make 59 changes in the document. And so a sixth schema on religious liberty was born. The new child was presented to the Council Fathers by Bishop De Smedt, probably the most patient servant of the bishops at the Council. On November 19, 1965 out of 2216 bishops, 1954 voted positively, and 249 negatively, with 13 invalid votes for what became the Declaration on Religious Freedom (*Dignitatis Humanae*) of Vatican II.

The *Council Daybook*, a daily report of conciliar proceedings, summarized Father John Courtney Murray's thoughts as follows:

> The exact point of controversy in the council on religious liberty is not whether it is rational in political and legal spheres, but whether the concept is mature enough at this point to link it up with the theological and moral spheres. The area of controversy is relatively narrow. [16]

The concept of respect for the human person so eloquently expressed by Pope John XXIII in his encyclical *Pacem in Terris*, was further deepened and clarified because the Declaration on Religious Freedom, as one commentator put it:

> constitutes by itself a genuine development of doctrine, perhaps the greatest and most characteristic progress achieved by the Council. [17]

In other words, "what was unhappily delayed was happily perfected," as Father John Courtney Murray observed at dinner with Cardinal Meyer at our Chicago House of Studies.

FOOTNOTES

(For full citations of sources, please see the Bibliography)

1. *Council Daybook*, Vol. 3, p. 162.
2. *America*, Nov. 30, 1963, p. 704.
3. *The Way*, 1985, Vol. 1, p. 312.
4. Abbott, p. 673.
5. Rynne, *The Second Session*, p. 223.
6. Ibid., p. 228.
7. *Commentary*, Vol. 4, p. 51.
8. Rynne, *The Third Session*, pp. 259-260.
9. *Council Daybook*, Vol. 1, p. 149.
10. *Council Daybook*, Vol. 2, p. 36.
11. Yzermans, p. 653.
12. Ibid., p. 651.
13. *Council Daybook*, Vol. 2, p. 37.
14. Ibid.
15. Ibid.
16. Ibid., p. 46.
17. *Commentary*, Vol. 4, p. 62.

X.

The Church And The World

Schema 13, on the Church, the World and Man, was the most talked-about and most long-awaited schema of Vatican II. It formally became *Gaudium et Spes*, the Pastoral Constitution on the Church in the Modern World. It was a fitting document to bring the Council to a close, and was an answer to Pope John's dream that at long last the Church would open herself to the world and interpret her message to it. It was also the fulfillment of what Pope Paul VI envisioned for the Council. As Pope John's successor, he built well and wisely to fulfill that dream.

On December 25, 1961, in the papal document, *Humanae Salutis* which announced the convocation of the Second Vatican Council, Pope John XXIII had these words:

> It is a question in fact of bringing the modern world into contact with the vivifying and perennial energies of the Gospel, a world which exalts itself with its conquests in the technical and scientific fields but which brings also the consequences of a temporal order which some have wished to reorganize excluding God. . . . This supernatural order must, however, reflect its efficiency in the other order, the temporal one, which on so many occasions is unfortunately the only one that occupies and worries man. [1]

It is in this context that the now well-known expression "the signs of the times" is implied by the Pope as his expression of what he felt the Council should be all about. He later used the expression more vividly in his encyclical *Pacem in Terris* in April, 1963. It was a reading of those ''signs of the times'' by the bishops called to Vatican II that moved them to enter into a dialogue with the world and to express their feelings in their very first public act, their message to humanity on October 20, 1962. In that message the bishops promised to work for peace and social justice and stressed that:

> We wish to convey to all men and to all nations the message of salvation, love and peace which Jesus Christ, Son of the living God, brought to the world and entrusted to the Church. . . . Under the guidance of the Holy Spirit, we intend in this meeting to seek the most effective ways of renewing ourselves and of becoming increasingly more faithful witnesses of the Gospel of Christ. . . . United here from every nation under heaven, we carry in our hearts the anxieties of all peoples entrusted to us, the anxieties of body and soul, sorrows and desires, and hopes. We turn our minds constantly toward all the anxieties afflicting men today.[2]

But there is another fascinating background to the Pastoral Constitution on the Church in the Modern World. It is the one document that came out of the Council itself. Many bishops alluded to the necessity of the Church looking to the problems of the world in the preparatory phases of the Council, but it was one of their confreres who put flesh on the idea and won over the support of the Pope—who, as already indicated, did not want the Church in Council just looking in on herself.

In the early part of 1962, the Cardinal Archbishop of Malines, Leo Suenens, had addressed a pastoral letter to his flock in which he expressed his own anxieties on the relationship of the Church to the world. He hoped that he would find among his confreres at the forthcoming Council an open mind to the problems of the world with which he was so concerned. Little did he realize that his letter would reach the hands of his friend Pope John XXIII. The Pope

later selected the Cardinal as a special envoy to the United Nations
to present before that august body his peace encyclical *Pacem in
Terris.*

After the Pope had studied Cardinal Suenens' letter, he called
him to Rome and told him how closely his ideas agreed with his
own about the future Council. Then he placed a further burden
upon his friend. He asked Cardinal Suenens to prepare a report on
the aims and organization of the Council soon to convene. The
Cardinal did so and submitted two important memoranda: one on
what the Council ought not, in his opinion, to be; and another
which approached the problem from a positive side. As Father
Charles Moeller, one of the theologians who worked on the text of
Schema 13, put it:

> It is not indiscreet now to state that the allocution of September 11,
> 1962 [Pope John's radio address on the Council] largely drew its
> inspiration from the second of these notes, so much so that John
> XXIII the next day made the Cardinal a present of one of his books
> as a sign of his agreement and gratitude.[3]

Pope John had consistently looked at the Council from three
viewpoints: The Church, the other Christian communities, and the
entire human family. The document *Humanae Salutis*, in which the
Pope had convoked the Council, demonstrated that same progression of viewpoints. The radio message of September 11 not only
showed his concern for the temporal problems the Council ought to
take up, but placed in even clearer light his other concerns: the
fundamental equality of people in exercising their rights and duties
toward the whole family of nations, the sacred character of marriage, the correct religious and moral outlook toward procreation,
the emphasis on religious faith and unbelief in all its forms and the
problem of poverty. On the problem of peace he had this to say:

> The bishops, as shepherds of Christ's flock in all nations, will again
> interpret the concept of peace, not in its negative aspect alone, as
> forbidding armed battles, but in its positive requirements as well.[4]

All of this makes clear the progression of events that led up to Cardinal Suenens' incisive intervention on December 4, 1962, just a few days before the end of the first session of Vatican II. It was then generally understood that the Cardinal's speech that day set the theme for what became the Pastoral Constitution on the Church in the Modern World and that he was, in a way, speaking for the Pope.

The official press bulletin for the day circulated to the Council Fathers that evening stated simply that one of the speakers recalled that the Holy Father, in his discourse on September 11, had expressed the hope that the Council would present the Church to the world as the light of the nations. Was it coincidence that when the bishops were searching for a title for the Dogmatic Constitution on the Church, they chose the words *Lumen Gentium* — Christ is the Light of all Nations?

As summarized by Antoine Wenger, Cardinal Suenens said that:

> The Church must go forth to meet the expectant world, and then make known her response to the problems that confront all men today, concerned as they are about respect for the human person, the inviolability of all life, procreation, social justice, the third force in international affairs, the evangelization of the poor, peace and war, so that the Church's doctrine may shine brightly as the light that lightens the nations. For the Church is not only responsible for her own members; she must also give thought to the separated Christians and undertake a dialogue with the world, in accordance with the orientations given by the Sovereign Pontiff in his message of September 11th and repeated in his opening address to the Council on the 11th of October.[5]

Like Cardinal Suenens, the then Archbishop of Milan, Giovanni Battista Montini, who later was to become Pope Paul VI, had been active in promoting this concept. In his traditional talk to the University of Milan in 1962 he said that the Council was of course devoting special attention to the modern world, with which she must increasingly engage in dialogue. In January 1963, in addressing a group of young priests, Cardinal Montini said:

> After twenty centuries of history, the Church seems to be submerged by profane civilization and to be absent from the contemporary world. While it is undertaking the task of defining itself, the Church is also looking for the world and trying to come in contact with that society.[6]

It was no surprise, therefore, that following on Cardinal Suenens' intervention of December 4, the Archbishop of Milan supported him.

Another potent impulse in favor of the schema on the Church in the Modern World came from the humble apostle of the poor, Dom Helder Camara, the Auxiliary Bishop of Rio de Janeiro. When the idea first began to be broached in the aula, Bishop Camara could be seen moving about St. Peter's talking with small groups of his confreres who came from the Third World. His favorite question with any group that would listen to him was: "Are we to continue spending all our time on the internal problems of the Church while two-thirds of the world is starving?" To pursue the answer to his question he brought together the secretaries of conferences from Africa, Japan, India, the Congo, and for strength, those from France, Holland, Germany and Canada. And then, at the suggestion of that little group he brought together, he made contact with Cardinal Suenens. No two unlike people made an alliance that was so effective.

On December 6, 1962, Cardinal Lercaro of Bologna, Italy, capped the intensive efforts of Suenens, Montini and Camara by not only supporting their views but by stating the essential spirit of the Council in these words (as summarized by Antoine Wenger):

> Now we understand more perfectly what the Council must accomplish in proclaiming the mystery of Christ, the Word of God, living and working within the Church. Now the mystery of Christ in His Church was always, and more than ever before is today, the

mystery of Christ in the poor. . . . Poverty is the sign of the Incarnation, proclaimed and foretold by the prophets, apparent in the Mother of God who was its servant in Bethlehem. We see it all during the public life of the Savior, and in the preaching of the Kingdom.[7]

Of the 73 schemata studied by the Council's Preparatory Commission, only the seventh one had anything to do with the social order. That schema had come out of the Theological Commission, which together with the Commission on the Apostolate of the Laity, was more concerned with the concept of "social action," a term already outdated prior to the calling of Vatican II. However, we must keep in mind that various elements of Christian social teaching were scattered among the other documents presented to the Council.

On December 5, 1962, just three days before the Council's first session was to adjourn, the bishops were given a booklet listing the 73 schemata. They were told, however, that the list had already been reduced to 17 and that the various commissions of the Council had been charged with the responsibility of reducing the number still further. As it turned out, the last of those schemata, the 17th, once the "mysterious" Schema 13, became the now famous Pastoral Constitution on the Church in the Modern World.

So the first session of Vatican II ended with an opening to the world. During the early part of 1963, and particularly during the summer of that year, as I mentioned earlier, a number of individuals and groups worked hard at trying to refine the texts that came out of the debates of the first session of the Council. Pope John XXIII added significantly to the clarification of that work with the issuance of his encyclical *Pacem in Terris* on April 11, 1963.

However, some of those involved with the work on Schema 17 felt that although *Pacem in Terris* intensified the interest of many countries in regard to what the Council would do about the problems of peace and social justice, it put the working group in a kind of dilemma since it had preempted the task they were assigned to do. In the final analysis, *Pacem in Terris* helped them by giving an example of language that did not need to be overly biblical or theological. More than that, it really provided greater interest in what should come out of the Council.

Toward the end of January, 1963, the Coordinating Commission of the Council (a kind of executive committee that represented the Council between sessions) was struggling with a "mixed bag" of preparatory texts for possible use in the schema on the Church in the Modern World. Cardinal Suenens (who served on that Commission) suggested that for reasons of expediency, a Mixed Commission of theologians and other experts be appointed to sift through those texts. By March, that Commission produced the very first text of the schema on the Church in the Modern World. A second text soon followed. Interest continued to mount, so much so, that the Coordinating Commission took the extraordinary step of setting up an Extra-Conciliar Commission under the chairmanship of Cardinal Suenens to handle Schema 17.

During September of 1963, Cardinal Suenens brought his Commission together at Malines, Belgium, with specific instructions from the Coordinating Commission in Rome that the draft of texts one and two be redone. That brought about text number three. Interestingly enough, this third text included the involvement of some 23 lay persons who were responsible for making the draft more understandable.

The first point raised was: To whom is the schema addressed? It was decided to speak to all Christians and to all men of good will, with the aim of bringing the light of the Lord to them, so that they may rightly understand the realities of this world, whose Lord has chosen a people for himself and given it the task of spreading his gospel.[8]

The group considered a wide range of problems:

> . . . for the first time the unification of the world has become possible, there is real solidarity, we can speak of a new humanity, a new experience of society and of love. At the same time there is the problem of class, labor and the poor; there is a will to justice which often becomes a source of atheism. Consequently the Church and Christians must "hear what the world has to say."
>
> Similarly, the duality of the present development of the world was brought out; unification, but also divisions which lead practically to civil war or to actual wars between nations; dominion over this world but also "ensnarement in the elements of this world"; freedom, a privilege of divine origin, but also its abuse, particularly by sin, which is a choice of evil for its own sake.
>
> In this way a double tension was discovered, between the Church as a heavenly structure founded on the word of God, on the one hand, and the world which is developing, growing together and seeking true justice on the other. There is also a tension within the world itself, between positive and negative aspects of its own evolution.
>
> Gradually a synthesis was arrived at. On the one hand, Christians need not accept the world as it is. On the contrary they should build it up in the light of the principles of their faith, for example in accordance with the command to fill the earth and subdue it (K. Rahner). On the other hand, it is "not necessary to reduce the role of humanity to that of a laybrother in a monastery" (Congar). A type of presence of the Church in the world must be achieved which is not one of power and domination but of service. And this kind of presence should also guarantee the principle of free access to the gospel without compulsion of any kind.[9]

During the early part of 1964 continuing work on the drafts of Schema 17 converged in Rome, where the members of the Theological Commission and the Commission on the Apostolate of the Laity came up with a treatment that reflected more a study of "the signs of the times." This expression came from Pope John's encyclical *Pacem in Terris*, and it eventually became the essential theme for those who worked on the schema. The "Malines" texts had already been submitted to the Mixed Commission and also now reflected the same approach.

In regard to the expression, "the signs of the times," Charles Moeller has this to say:

> The expression comes from *Pacem in Terris*. The suggestion had already been made that it should serve as a guideline for the appendix chapters. It now appeared in the main text intended for presentation to the Council. It had a strange fate. On the one hand it was strongly criticized, particularly by some WCC observers (letter of 29 May 1964), because biblically it has a very special, eschatological meaning, and this almost completely disappears in the context of the new paragraph. This involves, they argued, the danger of reading history in a human way and of indulging in prophetic exegesis of events. In the end the term disappeared completely, emerging only once in the final text (art. 4), where it is made clear that these signs are to be read in the light of the gospel. [10]

In the early part of June 1964, the Mixed Commission had a "ready" text and submitted it to the Coordinating Commission of the Council. On June 26, that Commission felt the text was ready for mailing to the Council Fathers. Pope Paul approved and within the month it was in the hands of the bishops all over the world who would bring that text with them to Rome for the third session of Vatican II.

On August 6, Pope Paul VI issued his first encyclical *Ecclesiam Suam*, which not only had a great impact on the preparation for debate in the Council on the document on the Church in the Modern World, but gave the bishops further encouragement to take seriously this new "openness to the world." The encyclical (which, like *Pacem in Terris* was addressed to "all men of good will") went further, and was at the heart of article 2 of the Pastoral Constitution on the Modern World, which reads:

Hence this Second Vatican Council, having probed more profoundly into the mystery of the Church, now addresses itself without hesitation, not only to the sons of the Church and to all who invoke the name of Christ, but to the whole of humanity. For the Council yearns to explain to everyone how it conceives of the presence and activity of the Church in the world of today.

And so, on September 14, 1964, the bishops converged on Rome for the opening of the third session of Vatican II. During that session the bishops would devote a good deal of their energy to consideration of the relationship between the Church, the world and man. Despite their growing suspicion that some wanted to abandon the schema on the Church in the Modern World, and that a few others wished to replace it with a simple declaration, they soon realized that:

> the world would not understand how the bishops could spend three sessions studying their own position in the Church but could not find time for serious study of the problems of two-thirds of mankind.[11]

On October 20, at the 105th general meeting of Vatican II, the much talked-about and long-awaited provisional text on the Church and the Modern World was presented for debate. Before the sixth and final schema would be approved more than a year later, some 20,000 observations comprising 830 pages would be made. There would be 169 oral interventions during the 13 meetings that the document was discussed. And again, concern would be voiced that coming so late in the third session of the Council, consideration of the text would be given short shrift, or that it would be relegated to a fourth session of the Council, were there to be one. There was even the rumor that the schema might be withdrawn from any debate in order to allow the Council to end with a third session.

But as history would have it, a strong protest prepared by a small group of Cardinals and presented to the Pope stemmed any scuttling of the Schema. As Xavier Rynne put it:

> It is unthinkable that Pope Paul himself can have seriously entertained the idea of side-tracking the document, since he, as Cardinal Montini, along with Pope John and Cardinal Suenens, had been one of its prime movers from the very start. [12]

Perhaps the most significant intervention made in the early stages of the debate on the document on the Church and the Modern World, the one that confirmed its future and delineated its theological aim, was that of Cardinal Meyer of Chicago, who called for the compenetration of the Church into the world. The Cardinal echoed the words of Pope John XXIII, who in his *Journal of a Soul* insisted that we must "infect the world with Christ." Cardinal Meyer used these words:

> The schema explains in different ways why the Christian living in the world ought to work for the advancement of the temporal order. Yet it does not adequately explain why man's daily work constitutes an integral part of the economy of salvation. We should not forget that God offers the hope of glory not just to man's soul, but to his whole person and to the entire world. No one denies that, along the way, man fairly often misuses the world and the good things that make it up. But the schema is too preoccupied with this danger. It is too fearful of infection from the world and too strong in urging the Christian to pass his life as "one departing and about to pass on." This preoccupation, which seems excessive to me, is the result (unless I am mistaken) of a certain omission, and not an insignificant one, in the schema. For nowhere does the schema plainly make known that element of Christian revelation which every kind of false dualism denies: namely, that the whole world is not only the means by which redeemed man perfects himself, but is itself the object of redemption, just as our bodies are. [13]

The Cardinal's intervention reminded me of this sentence from *Ecclesiam Suam*:

> Since the world cannot be saved from the outside, we must first of
> all identify ourselves with those to whom we would bring the
> Christian message — like the Word of God who Himself became a
> man (#87).[14]

As was later observed by several of the Council's experts, this
one and only intervention of Cardinal Meyer on Schema 13 had the
most influence on its fifth and sixth (final) versions and continued
to dominate the theological horizons of that document. The Cardinal died on April 9, 1965 and never witnessed the impact of his
intervention.

The only dissenter to the general acceptability of the text under
consideration during the third session of the Council was Cardinal
Ruffini of Palermo in Italy — who, by the way, was a very good
and long-time friend of Cardinal Meyer. The Italian prelate felt that
the text was obscure, was filled with flaws and weakened by
repetition. One of the obscurities he felt was its stress on the
humanitarian mission of the Church almost to the exclusion of her
main mission to procure eternal salvation. He also felt that the text
exaggerated the idea of dialogue in ecumenism. He went so far as
to ask for an entire revision of the text in accord with the encyclicals
of modern Popes.

Very quickly, one of Ruffini's compatriots, Cardinal Lercaro
of Bologna, stood up to caution the Fathers not to fear the difficulties inherent in the text and reminded them that the Council
was committed to produce a document of this kind. Bowing toward
Cardinal Ruffini he said: ''We must expect contradictory viewpoints and we must face them.'' The most violent attack, however,
couched in some of the strongest language ever used in the
Council, came from Britain's ranking prelate, Archbishop John
Heenan:

> What sort of judgment, venerable brothers, do you think the
> world will pass on this treatise? On some questions, as we know, it
> is better to say too little than too much. On the subject of world

problems, however, it would have been much better to say nothing than produce a set of platitudes. I would like you to call to mind the number of sittings we had when the question of the sources of Revelation was so fiercely debated. The theologians, of course, rightly regarded this as a highly important topic. But to the citizens of the wide world, whether Catholic or non-Catholic, a debate of this kind seems like wasting time and beating the air. Having spent such a long time on theological niceties this council will become a laughing-stock in the eyes of the world, if it now rushes breathlessly through a debate on world hunger, nuclear war and family life. People will ask ironically and with good reason what do we really mean when we call this a pastoral council?

I must speak plainly. This document is going to dash the hopes of everyone who has been awaiting it. Its authors do not seem to realize even to whom the message should be directed. Here is an example of their way of writing: "Christians," they say, "are ready to engage in a dialogue with all men of good will." But surely this is a pointless thing to say. Christians should be ready to conduct a dialogue with anyone whether or not he is a man of good will. The whole treatise reads more like a sermon than a document of a council. [15]

Archbishop Heenan went so far as to suggest that the Council be delayed for four years in order that a new commission of laity and priests "with pastoral experience" be allowed to work on the social problems brought up in the document.

Sustained laughter greeted the Archbishop's intervention and again Cardinal Lercaro, who was in the chair that day, amid sustained applause, brought the Council discussions back to a more even keel.

Subsequent debate on the text revolved around four points:

One was the reason for the relative silence of the text in regard to atheism. Text 6, the final one, as we shall see later, ignored the well-organized move of a certain group of bishops who wanted to include express condemnation of Marxist communism.

The second point raised by some bishops brought out the

question of why the Church should speak of earthly things at all. Again some of the bishops around me cringed. One of my neighbors, a bishop from Canada, said: "Seems like those men have not yet read *Ecclesiam Suam*."

The third point concerned the person and the family and whatever effects racial discrimination would have on them. That subject received much attention later when the fourth chapter of the document, titled "Marriage and Family," was presented to the bishops by Archbishop Dearden of Detroit.

The fourth area of concern, brought up by a number of the Council Fathers, had to do with culture, development, peace and atomic weapons. The subject of nuclear warfare caused some consternation. It was introduced late in the Council's deliberations on the schema on the Church and the Modern World. A letter on nuclear warfare circulated by Auxiliary Bishop Philip Hannan of Washington, D.C. (who was supported by five other American prelates as well as seven from other countries) had little effect on the debates in that fourth area. Apparently, many of the bishops were "turned off" by the strong wording of the letter. In substance the letter asked the Council Fathers to vote "no" on a war and peace statement unless "errors" were corrected. If those errors (the claim was that the specific section of the schema smacked too much of pacifism) were not corrected, the signatories went so far as to suggest that the Fathers vote "no" in the final balloting on the entire document, and that the whole matter of the Church and the Modern World be turned over the the next Synod of Bishops.

This radical proposal unfortunately brought about unnecessary, prolonged and heated debates.

> Fortunately the crisis which might have prevented the final vote on the whole Pastoral Constitution was overcome by an explanatory note which was proposed by Msgr. Garrone and approved by the Mixed Commission. It showed that the anxiety of the American bishops was unfounded and that the text was less unqualified than it appeared.[16]

Another member of the Mixed Commission, Bishop Marcos McGrath of Panama, at a press conference stated that:

> The statement on possession or accumulation of nuclear weapons has been dropped from the final version because it was decided that "rather than [sic.] getting into the prudential area of weapons without complete knowledge of military objectives" would be beyond the Council's competence. [17]

Pope Paul's speech to the United Nations in October of 1965 put the whole subject of nuclear armament more prudently and realistically, and this view was reflected in the final text of the Pastoral Constitution on the Church in the Modern World.

Frantic telephone exchanges between the bishops themselves and between bishops and theologians, soon after Pope Paul VI returned from the United Nations and addressed the Council, made it possible to put the final text of the schema on the Church and the Modern World to a vote on October 6 and 7, 1965.

One of the most heartening interventions, made just before the final vote, was greeted with enthusiasm and an outpouring of charity and respect for a true servant of the Church. Cardinal Ottaviani, the Head of the Holy Office, received a warm and prolonged ovation, when in a vibrant and emotion-filled voice he urged the Council to summon all nations to a one-world republic that would end the threat of nuclear doom. The venerable and almost blind Cardinal asserted the duty and the right of people to reject even their own legal government if it is leading them into a ruinous war.

On October 29, 1964, the Council began discussion of the crucial subject of marriage and birth control. The bishops, well aware of the confusion among their flocks, and realizing that they needed to return to their dioceses with answers, gave these two subjects their rapt attention. Even the coffee bars began to be less frequented as speaker after speaker was greeted with enthusiastic

:spite the fact that the Pope had reserved to himself a
the question of family limitation.

Archbishop Dearden of Detroit presented for the Commission
this section of the schema and reported the Holy Father's decision
to set up a special commission to study the complicated subject of
family limitation.

> This document, as drafted by the commission, lays down the
> principle that fecundity in marriage should be both generous and
> conscious, Archbishop Dearden said.
>
> Judgment about how many children a couple should have be-
> longs to the partners in the marriage, he said. Their decision on
> whether to restrict the number of children should be made with a
> correctly formed conscience.
>
> Judgment about the means of limiting offspring, he said, must
> be made according to the mind of the Church. [18]

The Archbishop went on to explain that discussion of the use of
the pill for limiting births was avoided not only because the Pope
had reserved that question to himself, but because it was such an
intricate problem that discussion on the Council floor would be
unable to settle it.

However, since the floor was open to general discussion of
marriage and the family, specific references to the problem of birth
control came up none the less. The bishops were not to be denied
their day in court. Cardinal Suenens of Belgium opened the door to
further discussion of the subject. He presented, however, a new
and fresh approach. He was voicing, in a prophetic way, some of
the language that later appeared in *Humanae Vitae*, the encyclical
on birth control of Pope Paul VI that came out in 1968.

The Cardinal felt that the Church needed to penetrate every
angle of research on the subject of birth control. Although he
cautioned that there is ''no question of modifying or of doubting the
truly traditional teachings of the Church,'' there is no reason why
the Church cannot make a thorough inquiry into the subject.

Modern science, he said, may have much to tell us in this regard. Here, the Cardinal was echoing what would later appear in article 24 of *Humanae Vitae*. Cardinal Suenens stated: "I implore you, brothers, let us avoid another Galileo trial. One is enough for the Church."[19]

Cardinal Suenens was applauded for this presentation, as was Cardinal Leger of Canada, who put his thoughts on that delicate subject in another way:

> He noted that some people seem to fear any revision of the theology of marriage. They fear the Church will be accused of opportunism in undertaking such a study. But, he said, we cannot forget that this review has been provoked by the worries of some of the faithful and that its only purpose is to protect the holiness of marriage.[20]

More applause greeted the Melkite Patriarch of Antioch, Maximos IV Saigh, who put Cardinal Suenens' thoughts more bluntly when he said that:

> There is here a conflict between the official doctrine of the Church and the contrary practice of the vast majority of Christian families. The authority of the Church is once more questioned on a large scale. . . . Frankly, should not the official positions of the Church regarding this matter be revised in the light of modern science, theological as well as medical, psychological and sociological?[21]

The old view of marriage on the part of many Catholics (that is, that couples were to have as many children as possible) was already changed in practice before the bishops at the Council began to discuss the subject. However, the applause that greeted the speakers indicated that there was need for authoritative backing for some kind of change.

When the first interventions on racism and discrimination came up at the Council, and many bishops spoke on those subjects, the question of women in society and in the Church came up. The African and Canadian bishops were the first to plead for recognition of the dignity of women. Bishop Gerard Coderre of Quebec,

Canada was among the first who said that the growing recognition of the dignity of women in the world was among those "signs of the times" that must be studied and included in the schema on the Church in the Modern World. He emphasized that men should not only give women their proper place in the world, but recognize that they are necessary for the completion of the divine plan for man's perfection, for the perfection of the family and of society in general.

How prophetic were the words of Augustin Frotz, Auxiliary Bishop of Cologne, Germany who said:

> The Church has not yet become aware of the world-wide implications of the changed position of women in modern society. Women should be accepted as the Church's grown-up daughters, not just children. In the liturgy they should be addressed directly as "sisters," and not just submerged in the salute "brothers."[22]

In another intervention almost a year later, during the fourth and last session of the Council, the same Bishop Frotz:

> called on the council to state not only the equality between men and women, but also to outline the unique role each must play in the development of culture. The fact that men and women play roles complementary to each other is in the order of nature, he said. Therefore, it should not be confined to marriage, but extend into every order of human existence.[23]

At a press conference that evening which I attended, I heard Cardinal Suenens say that it was about time the Church abandoned her masculine superiority complex. We must not only respect woman's true dignity but learn to appreciate her part in the plan of God. But probably the strongest and most significant comment made about women at the Council was that of Archbishop Paul Hallinan, of Atlanta, Georgia. As summarized in the *Council Daybook*, his talk went as follows:

In a statement filed with the council's general secretariat, the American prelate declared that since women "constitute half the people of God" they should be given equal consideration in the council's schema on the Church in the modern world.

The archbishop asked whether the Church "has given the leadership that Christ, by word and example, clearly showed he expected of her."

"In proclaiming the equality of man and woman the Church must act as well as speak by fraternal testimony, not only in abstract doctrine," he said.

Therefore, "every opportunity should be given women, both Religious and lay, to offer their special talents to the service of the Church, and their role of auditors in the present council must be only the beginning."

Specifically, Archbishop Hallinan recommended that:

In liturgical functions women should be permitted to act as lectors and acolytes at Mass;

Women after proper study and formation should be allowed to serve as deaconesses by preaching and in providing those sacraments which deacons do, especially Baptism and the distribution of Holy Communion;

Women also should be encouraged to become teachers and consultants in theology when they have attained competence in the field;

Women should be included in whatever organization is established for the post-conciliar implementation of the lay apostolate;

Women Religious should be fully represented and consulted, at least in all matters concerning their interests, in the Congregation of Religious and in the commission revising canon law.

In his statement, Archbishop Hallinan referred to a statement made in 1961 by Pope Paul VI when he was Archbishop of Milan, which reads: "Women must come closer to the altar, to souls and to the Church in order to gather together the people of God."

Archbishop Hallinan said the "community between man and woman" mentioned in the schema on the Church in the modern world "should not be one of subservience but one of harmony, mutual respect, love and responsibility." Therefore, "we must not continue to perpetuate the secondary place accorded to women in the Church of the 20th century. We must not continue to be late-comers in the social, political and economic development that has today reached climactic conditions."

In our society, he explained, "women in many places and in many respects still bear the marks of inequality.

"This is evident in working conditions, wages and hours of work, in marriage and property laws. Above all it is present in that gradualism, bordering on inaction, which limits their presence in the tremendous forces now working for universal education, for peace, for the rehabilitation of the deprived, the just and compassionate care of the young, the aged and the needy, the dispossessed and the victims of human injustice and weakness."

As for the Church, Archbishop Hallinan said, "her history . . . has been a struggle to free women from the old place of inferiority. Her great women saints, her dedicated virgins, her defense of woman in the family, a few women theologians, but especially the unique honor given by her to God's only perfect creature, Mary Our Lady — all these are part of that history."

"But the Church has been slow in denouncing the degradation of women in slavery, and in claiming for them the right of suffrage and economic equality," he said.

"Particularly, the Church has been slow to offer women, in the selection of their vocations, any choice but that of mother or nun. In fact, among her saints, there are only three groups: martyrs, virgins, and a vague, negative category called 'neither virgins, nor martyrs.' "[24]

As I went through the documents of Vatican II, I could not help but notice that in the Decree on the Apostolate of the Laity there is this reference to women:

Since in our times women have an ever more active share in the whole life of society, it is very important that they participate more widely also in the various fields of the Church's apostolate (#9).

However, in the Pastoral Constitution on the Church in the Modern World, there is sparse mention of the role of women in the Church and in society despite some 16 interventions similar to the ones I referred to above. Woman is mentioned just four times in the whole of the Constitution, except where she enters the category of "man." A sentence in that document reflects this bland treatment in these words:

> Women are now employed in almost every area of life. It is appropriate that they should be able to assume their full proper role in accordance with their own nature (#60).

This was despite Pope Paul's declared intention of bringing women into the Council's deliberations. In his opening talk to the third session of the Council he said:

> And we are delighted to welcome among the auditors our beloved daughters in Christ, the first women in history to participate in a conciliar assembly. [25]

There was no doubt, as the third session of Vatican II ended, that the schema on the Church in the Modern World, which survived three weeks of intensive discussions, would be subject to drastic revision. As was indicated earlier, the feeling among the Council Fathers persisted that it did not present an adequate theology of the Church and the world. But this was not surprising. After all, this was the first time the Church in council sought a contemporary theology on such a complex of problems that affected the world and the Church's relationship to it. Pope John XXIII did ask the bishops to "study the signs of the times" — but that was easier said than done.

At the close of the third session on November 21, 1964, Pope Paul VI, in his farewell address, spoke of the work still to be done. About the schema on the Church and the World he said that:

The Church is for the world. The Church seeks no other earthly power for herself than that which will make it possible for her to serve and to love. As she perfects her thought and structure, the Church does not aim to separate herself from the experience of individual men but rather endeavors to understand them better while sharing their sufferings and their aspirations. This place of the Church in the world, studied and discussed already in this session, will find its complete development in the next and last session. [26]

Throughout the whole of the month of February, 1965, an enlarged steering committee of 39 theologians and Council periti, as well as 20 lay persons worked on the revised text of what was Schema 17 (formerly the famous Schema 13) in Ariccia, near Rome. By April they had hammered out a text that won the approval of the Central Coordinating Commission. Pope Paul VI authorized the mailing of this new 80-page text to the world's bishops on May 11.

During the fourth and final session of Vatican II, discussion of the Ariccia text on the Church and the Modern World dominated the meetings of the bishops from September 22 to October 8, 1965. More than 163 Council Fathers gave oral and written interventions. It is interesting to note that over the long history of the document more than 20,000 suggestions were made. The periti (and other experts involved from time to time) took serious note of all these suggestions and surprisingly enough came up with two large booklets for the bishops to study. On November 12 and 13, 1965, after study and discussion by the bishops, the "new text" became the *textus recognitus* (the revised text). New "modi," or interventions by the bishops caused another text to be produced, the final *textus denuo recognitus* (the text again revised).

The day before the Council ended, 2373 Council Fathers present cast 2309 affirmative votes for the final text of Schema 17. Pope Paul, with the bishops, promulgated the now famous and much debated Pastoral Constitution on the Church in the Modern World, and from its opening words called it *Gaudium et Spes*, the "Joys and Hopes."

As in the past, the eloquent Coadjutor Bishop of Strasbourg, France, Leon Elchinger, had captured the meaning of this document. As summarized in the *Council Daybook*:

> The ecumenical council was urged to keep in mind the intention of Pope John XXIII to show the world a renewed face of the Church that would attract all men by the splendor of Christ's teaching.[27]

On December 7, 1965, the day before the Council came to a close, Pope Paul VI gave a similar message to the bishops and special delegations from all parts of the world:

> Never before, perhaps, so much as on this occasion has the Church felt the need to know, to draw near to, to understand, to penetrate, serve and evangelize the society in which she lives and to come to grips with it, almost to run after it in its rapid and continuous change.[28]

In the prayers of the faithful, at the closing Mass of the Second Vatican Council, this intercession, among others, echoed throughout the hall of St. Peter's Basilica:

> That the fruits which God has deigned to bestow on His Church through this ecumenical council may be studiously grasped with sincere and open minds by all of us. . .

FOOTNOTES

(For fuller citations of sources, please see the Bibliography)

1. *Council Daybook*, Vol. 1, pp. 6-7.
2. Ibid., p. 45.
3. *Commentary*, Vol. 5, p. 8.
4. Wenger, p. 216.
5. Ibid., pp. 123-124.

6. Congar, p. 25.
7. Wenger, p. 128.
8. *Commentary*, Vol. 5, p. 21.
9. Ibid., p. 22.
10. Ibid., p. 35.
11. Ibid., p. 40.
12. Rynne, *The Third Session*, p. 116.
13. Yzermans, p. 232.
14. *The Papal Encyclicals*, Vol. 5, p. 153.
15. *Council Daybook*, Vol. 2, p. 175.
16. *Commentary*, Vol. 5, p. 68.
17. *Council Daybook*, Vol. 3, p. 262.
18. *Council Daybook*, Vol. 2, p. 203.
19. Ibid., pp. 203-204, 208-209.
20. Ibid., p. 204.
21. Ibid., p. 209.
22. Ibid., p. 205.
23. *Council Daybook*, Vol. 3, p. 88.
24. Ibid., pp. 118-119.
25. *Council Daybook*, Vol. 2, p. 10.
26. Ibid., pp. 300, 305.
27. *Council Daybook*, Vol. 3, p. 53.
28. Ibid., p. 281.

XI.

Hope For The Future

Hope for the future Church, as I interpret the "signs of the times," strongly depends on how well the leaders who serve the Church will follow the Spirit that brought about Vatican II. That Council saw the Church as standing on the frontier of a new age in her history, and it saw co-responsibility and freedom to be important ingredients of this.

As a priest and as a bishop I was a product of the pre-conciliar Church. I attended all of the sessions of the Second Vatican Council and sincerely tried to be part of its prophetic witness to the Church and to the world. As the ordinary of a diocese, I was given the opportunity of implementing — with the help of some very talented people of that diocese — the documents of the Second Vatican Council.

For all of us in that local Church, renewal was a privileged time in our lives. Although the road was not easy for everyone and there were understandable differences, we shared a new manifestation of the Church as institution and as sacrament of our salvation.

Our local Church was essentially, like so many others, a clerically dominated Church. With time, it grew to become a Church of the People of God, that relished the excitement of change and direction, in which ministry and service became part of everyone's life. In that Church we took seriously Pope John's injunction to:

> give the Church the possibility to contribute more efficaciously to the solution of the problems of the modern age.[1]

To what extent those solutions may be brought about, as we move into the 21st century, will depend in large measure on how correctly and how vigorously the renewal brought about by the Second Vatican Council is pursued at all levels of the Church's life. Cardinal Basil Hume of England, at the Extraordinary Synod of Bishops in the fall of 1985, put that concern much more succinctly in these words:

> There is still a long way to go before the teachings of the Council enter fully into our Catholic bloodstream.[2]

My purpose for writing and sharing the experiences I had of Vatican II is to add something into that bloodstream, to entice the new ministries that have become so familiar a part of parish life (especially in the United States) to delve into the documents of Vatican II, study them and build on them the future Church.

Before and since the Second Vatican Council, there have been signposts along the way indicating that Pope John XXIII was on target in calling the bishops to Rome to "study the signs of the times," and to build on the foundations for change and renewal that were set many years before.

Long before the Council began its deliberations, scholars in various fields of learning had been at work to bring change to the Church — that is, renewal of her internal structure and new understanding of her relationship to the world. At the grassroots there was a hint that the "faithful" were ready for new responsibilities in the mission of the Church. Here and there, they were asking for a new structure, a new model of the Church. In the United States we were no longer an immigrant Church, but a Church in which the faithful — products of a thorough-going

Catholic education system — took on theological perspectives that influenced their commitment as Christians.

Thus, as the world's bishops gathered around the Pope, above St. Peter's tomb, in the historic setting of an Ecumenical Council that October of 1962, they brought with them that same sense of urgency and understanding of their roots and the need to find new nourishment for the Church they represented.

In the light of this atmosphere, the Catholic Church began the most profound religious event of the 20th century. Building on the work of scholars prior to the Council, the Church modernized and simplified her worship practices by stripping them of centuries of accretions that no longer spoke to the centrality of the Mass and the sacraments. She invited the faithful to a new (and in some cases, a surprising) familiarity with the sanctuary through use of the vernacular and active participation in the Eucharistic celebration. She provided a real discovery of the word of God as a living force for the Christian way of life, and demonstrated that the religions of the world have a common bond and interest.

Although reforms in the liturgy, Scripture studies and ecumenism were in many ways the more popular of the Council's achievements, they became the connecting threads for the most notable and revolutionary documents of that Council. The Dogmatic Constitution on the Church, for instance, reached back to 1871 and the First Vatican Council to not only finish discussion begun then on the inner nature of the Church as established by Christ, but added the new concept of collegiality and shared responsibility for her mission. It provided:

> a radically different vision of the Church, more biblical, more historical, more vital and dynamic.[3]

The other document, the Pastoral Constitution on the Church in the Modern World, provided the Church with a theology of the "signs of the times." It was born of the friendship of three men, Pope John XXIII, Cardinal Suenens and Pope Paul VI. Pope John asked the Cardinal to provide an agenda for the Council, and Pope Paul applied these thoughts to his first encyclical, *Ecclesiam Suam*, which deeply influenced the Pastoral Constitution.

In all of its sixteen documents, Vatican II emphasizes the Church, and this is understandable. After all, as I indicated earlier, the subject of the nature and mission of the Church was the unfinished business of Vatican I. The bishops who responded to Pope John's invitation to come to Rome, were aware of this. Little did they realize, however, that they would be providing a new concept of Church, one not exclusively centered in Rome, but in a community of faith, a People of God spread across a world over which the Risen Lord presides and leads the faithful to His Father.

Another important change sparked by Vatican II reflected Pope John's desire for "an inner renewal of the Church and its members," with emphasis on the image of the Church as the Body of Christ. As a matter of fact, the first eight articles of the Dogmatic Constitution on the Church provide exquisite examples of the Pauline teaching on this concept:

> Christ is the light of all nations. Hence this most sacred Synod, which has been gathered in the Holy Spirit, eagerly desires to shed on all men that radiance of His which brightens the countenance of the Church (#1).

> In that body, the life of Christ is poured into the believers, who, through the sacraments, are united in a hidden and real way to Christ who suffered and was glorified (#7).

And Father Karl Rahner, in writing about the future Church, emphasizes that her Christian spirituality:

> will need to be related to Christ the Crucified and Risen, in whose person there is the ultimate, victorious and irreversible promise of God historically manifested to the world.[4]

The historical significance, then, of the Dogmatic Constitution on the Church is that it built on the notion of a People to whom God communicates Himself in love by sharing His Son with the world.

The theology that permeates this document is dominated by a Christology based on the Gospel of St. John. This is so much the case, that the Christian spirituality of the future Church that Father Rahner writes about, will demand an individual relationship to Jesus. Otherwise, the Church may lose many members to those fundamentalist groups, so prolific in our day, that stress this personal relationship. In Father Rahner's reading of John 10:1, for instance, "The Church is a sheepfold where the one and the necessary door is Christ."

Christology, then, will need to dominate the theological thinking of the Church of the future. There will need to be carved out of the documents of Vatican II, ever more accurately, the foundation on which future Christian spirituality will depend. There will need to be an enrichment of our understanding of the Church as the Body of Christ, of how she precisely relates to our Lord and to ourselves.[5] Father Walter Kasper, the distinguished Christologist at the University of Tübingen in Germany states that:

Christ is the light of humanity. The Church, proclaiming the Gospel, must see to it that this light clearly shines out from her countenance. The Church makes herself credible if she speaks less of herself and ever more preaches Christ crucified and witnesses with her own life. The message of the Church, as described in the Second Vatican Council, is Trinitarian and Christocentric (Art. II A, 2).[6]

All this emphasis on the centrality of Christ in the Church of the future will of course have a significant impact on all our ministries, if only for the reason that each of us will have a different relationship to the Jesus of the Gospels and of history. Again, as Father Kasper writes:

The reality of the redemption through Jesus Christ is conveyed and made present through concrete encounters, conversations, living communion with human beings who are touched by Christ. [7]

And Bishop Christopher Butler, an influential participant in the Second Vatican Council, was prophetic when he said that:

The saving disclosure which God has given us is not merely truth about Christ, it is Christ himself in his person and in his being who will touch through us the lives of others. [8]

Here then is further indication that the Church is not simply an organization but a community of faith over which Christ must preside more intimately in the future and through whom the baptized will exercise their particular ministry in His name. This charismatic element in the Church must be recognized and must be distinguished from its institutional element because it belongs to the nature of the Church. In Father Rahner's words:

No, there are things in the Church which cannot be planned, which cannot be institutionalized and which are unexpected. . . . There is a charismatic element in the Church, as part of the Church, and only complete with this element is the Church what God wants her to be and what she also always will be through His Spirit. [9]

It is already evident today, and therefore should be more apparent in the future, that there are many people whose lives are empty; who are searching for meaning to their faith; who need to know Christ, His love, His mercy and forgiveness; who need to see not an institution or organization, but in each of us, now sharing the mission of the whole Church, a loving and caring Christ.

During the century since Vatican I, the Church had wrestled with a single fundamental issue: What is the significance of the secular world, of human life lived there, and of the Church's relationship to that world? There were, as I showed earlier, many pressures at the Second Vatican Council to come up with some solutions to this fundamental issue.

The longest document given us, therefore, by the Second Vatican Council, the Pastoral Constitution on the Church in the Modern World, offered many solutions to this fundamental issue. It is the document for the here and now of the Church and her future. It is unequaled in terms of how the Church will need to live in our world and bring the Kingdom of God into it. It came out of the Council and the concern of its assembled Fathers to be genuinely committed to the welfare of humanity. That commitment was beautifully expressed in the very first sentence of the Pastoral Constitution:

> The joys and the hopes, the griefs and the anxieties of the men of this age, especially those who are poor or in any way afflicted, are the joys and hopes, the griefs and anxieties of the followers of the Lord (#1).

Anthropology, ecclesiology and above all Christology were written into that document with clear directions for what the Church must be to humankind. Although solutions to human problems have been hard to come by since the Council ended in 1965, the principles are still there. The Church of the future will need to apply these principles with greater vigor if she is to be the credible witness of the presence of Christ to the world.

I believe that Pope John Paul II is trying to apply these principles by learning, at first hand, the condition of humankind in various parts of the world. Out of his experience he built on Pope Paul's encyclical, *Progressio Populorum*, which emphasized some of the more important themes of the Pastoral Constitution on the Church in the Modern World. His own encyclical, *Redemptor Hominis*, reflected that Constitution's treatment of the dignity of the human person.

And I believe that the Holy Father must have intervened in the controversy that surrounded the work of Father Leonardo Boff. A Franciscan priest in Brazil, his book, *Church: Charism and Power*, on liberation theology, tried to make real in his own country a Church centered in the People of God and not on herself. For that, he was reprimanded by the Sacred Congregation for the Doctrine of the Faith and not allowed to lecture or publish for a year. He was later exonerated in an unprecedented demonstration of solidarity and support on the part of two Brazilian Cardinals to whom the Holy Father must have listened, since he had met them on their own territory just a year before.

Father Boff, from my reading of his book, vigorously applied the principles of the Pastoral Constitution on the Church in the Modern World to the sad conditions that exist in Latin America and may have done so with too heavy an emphasis on the Church as a religious power controlled by the hierarchy in Rome. He did say that, because the Church's field of activity is strictly bound to the sacred, it is essentially a clerical Church based on official and orthodox formulas with a fixation on juridical-canonical aspects, and is therefore,

> insensitive to human problems that arise beyond its borders, in the world and in society.[10]

The Pastoral Constitution on the Church in the Modern World tried to remedy this sort of insensitivity. But one would suspect that Father Boff grew weary of waiting for the people in Rome to act on the implementation of this document to the same extent, for instance, that they acted on the Constitution on the Sacred Liturgy. One needs to remember that 23 post-conciliar documents followed on that latter Constitution. Then again, Father Boff may have applied in an unbalanced way Pope Paul VI's apostolic letter *Octogesima Adveniens* on social justice, which Father Yves Congar considered to be the model of the new way of exercising the pastoral magisterium.[11]

The insertion of the Church into the world by the Second Vatican Council brought about both a new understanding of the

separation between faith and life in our day, and a new development of doctrine best exemplified in the Declaration on Religious
Freedom. That development, as I mentioned in Chapter X, had a
profound effect on all the other documents of the Council. Bishop
Marcos McGrath of Panama, in a recent publication put it this way:

> The idea of starting from intellectual and social currents ("signs of
> the times") in order to reach doctrinal considerations was simply
> unknown and unrecognized as a possible way of proceeding, either
> for a Council, or for theologians, or in pastoral work.[12]

Today, perhaps because I share Father Boff's impatience — or
I might add, because I see signs that implementation of the Vatican
II documents or even the great encyclicals of Pope John XXIII and
Pope John Paul II is waning—I fear the future estrangement of the
People of God from their Church. More, for instance, needs to be
heard of the Dogmatic Constitution on Divine Revelation, which
fused the biblical view of history into the other two great documents of the Council, the Dogmatic and Pastoral Constitutions on
the Church. We must keep alive the inspiration of the Spirit that
moved the Fathers of the Council to the sources of faith in
Scripture, and in its light to tackle the problems of our day.

Who will do this? The answer is already at hand. In recent years
we have witnessed a vibrant growth of lay ministry alongside the
ordained ministry. This has been one of the blessings of the
post-conciliar Church. The laity in the United States, especially,
have come forward in increasing numbers to be of service in the
pastoral life of the Church. It is my conviction that the universality
of this call to take part in the Church's mission has important
implications especially for those who work in Christian education.
I mentioned earlier in this chapter that we are no longer an immigrant Church in the United States. Our Catholic school system,
supported at great sacrifice for more than a hundred years, has
produced theologically perceptive Christians ready, as article 31 of

the Dogmatic Constitution on the Church puts it, to ''carry out their own part in the mission of the whole Christian people with respect to the Church and the world.''

The Christian education of the young remains essential. It has become an important aspect of lay ministry today and may not be minimized. However, this ministry must not remain child-centered. The Church of the future will need to provide Catholic education that goes beyond childhood if the documents of Vatican II are to be understood and implemented correctly.

As I look back more than two decades after Vatican II, I must re-emphasize that most of its documents had little or no follow-up. We have reached a point in Church history at which it needs to be said that the Council created many expectations which have yet to be fulfilled.

There's been a progressive clouding of the significance of Vatican II. The ''heresy'' of the traditionalists who confuse resto-ration with renewal perdures. Although there was hope that the 1985 Extraordinary Synod of Bishops called by Pope John Paul II to assess the impact of the Council, provided some clearing of the air, the fact remains that this Synod did not generate formidable plans to bring the Council documents into life again. The Rev. Albert Outler, a Methodist theologian and observer at the Council, has this view with which I suspect many agree:

> We've been kept waiting for the council to come into clear focus — and it never has, not even when it was rehearsed and reaffirmed by that extraordinary synod. Every time one thinks of the so-called ''progressive'' orientation in the council as its main compass head-ing for the Catholic future . . . the die-hards reappear in the pilot house trying to head us back.[13]

On the positive side, however, I would want to emphasize that the Synod in the fall of 1985 did say that a new Church was emerging slowly, that today at least we are talking about people and not an institution, about a Church that is being reborn and that we are being reborn with her.

And in their second message the bishops celebrated not only the 20th anniversary of the Second Vatican Council, but also its verification and promotion. They emphasized again the central theme of the Council's teaching on collegiality. They expressed the hope that this new and refreshing spirit of fraternal cooperation between bishops, priests and people, this new emphasis on the apostolic role of the laity, on the priesthood of the faithful, and so many other doctrinal and pastoral developments that were at the heart of the Second Vatican Council might be woven into the rich fabric of the Church of the future.

Perhaps the most moving reverberation of the Council at the Synod was expressed with the prayer, that as the desire grew in the Church of the future on the part of the faithful who want to take part in the deliberations which shape their communities and their local Church, they would also acknowledge the centrality of Christ in their lives and in their work.

And reflecting on the general content of the reports which bishops brought with them from their National Conferences to the Synod, there was expressed the conviction that the Second Vatican Council was a gift from God to the Church and to the world; that it was a wellspring offered by the Holy Spirit to the Church for the present and the future.

Finally, there was the Pope's message to the bishops as they parted and made their way home. After praising them for the ''sensus ecclesiae,'' which dominated their message to the world, the Holy Father went on to urge them that:

> the great force and the awareness of the importance of the Council penetrate deeper into the universal Church, into your particular churches and into your various communities. [14]

There can be no doubt that as a result of the Second Vatican Council, now celebrated and confirmed by the Synod of 1985 as its authoritative interpreter, a new Church will emerge on the eve of the 21st century. Vatican II will bring to this Church new tasks and challenges etched deep in its documents. New traditions will emerge from new and unfamiliar materials. Christ will have to be found in places where we never looked before. His Church will need to walk beside people looking for religious experience in a world she never trod before. His gospel will need to penetrate our times.

The Church then will need to be in the world and not fear its "contamination." It will need to move forward in history because:

> The Lord is the goal of human history, the focal point of the longings of history and of civilization, the center of the human race, the joy of every heart, and the answer to all its yearnings (Pastoral Constitution on the Church in the Modern World, #45).

Granted, we bishops were confronted with a juridical form of ecclesiology (which after all was part of our heritage) when we arrived in Rome in the fall of 1962. But we came as pastors, and after four years we had learned a new language. The vocabulary of "power" and "hierarchy" disappeared, and we spoke rather of mission and service. The charismatic and participatory ministries of the People of God merged ever so easily with the affirmation of episcopal collegiality, and we knew that we had been manipulated by the Holy Spirit.

And therein is framed the Church of the future: a Church that is the People of God, the episcopate, the clergy, the religious, the laity, all sharing and living in the one body of Christ, discovering new ways of being Church, relishing the new charisms of grace and holiness.

Father Yves Congar used to like to emphasize in his lectures that:

> St. Paul did not found missions. He founded churches and these should not be transplanted but allowed to come to life and grow indigenously.[15]

That thought brings up another interesting accomplishment of Vatican II that will and must have a profound effect on the future of the Church. The principle of collegiality was fraught with misunderstanding in the beginning, but as the Council grew in stature it became the rallying force for much that is new today in ecclesiology. An important new direction for ecclesiology was the recognition of the reality and significance of the local Church. This, according to Father Congar,

> represents a movement away from an ecclesiology concerned simply with the universal Church and the expansion of one Church — the Church of Rome — throughout the world and forgetful of the reality of the local churches; in other words, an ecclesiology oriented towards a uniform universality which is pragmatically subdivided into dioceses. Karl Rahner believed that this was the most fundamentally new and the most promising contribution made by the Council. [16]

Although this new concept of the Church was not put into so many words, it pervaded the thinking of the Fathers at Vatican II. The Synod of 1985 brought this new definition of the Church to the fore out of "the chorus of the hemispheres" that dominated its deliberations. It gave a clear rendition of that chorus and indicated, as Vatican II did, an irreversible shift to a "world Church" as Karl Rahner conceived it.

Father Rahner's thesis of a "world Church" was, as I demonstrated earlier, clearly manifest (though at times hesitatingly) in the deliberations of Vatican II. Movements in the opposite direction, unfortunately, persist today—for example, in the centralized bureaucracy of the Roman Curia. But Pope John Paul II, on the occasion of the Extraordinary Synod of 1985, did emphasize a promise to realign the viewpoint of the Curia. After all, the agenda for that Synod came out of the deliberations of the National Conferences of Bishops whose representatives brought their thoughts to Rome.

It is a fact of history that European and North American Catholics no longer constitute the majority of the faithful. It is estimated that by the year 2000 over 70% of Catholics will be living in the so-called Third World countries. Father Alfred McBride makes this interesting observation:

> *Global Catholics.* The wheel of history is turning again. In the 1980's the smokestack industries of the industrial revolution are dying; the world of the microchip is being born. Brain power is replacing brawn power. In little over a century we have moved from the horse to the engine to the chip, from the farmer to the laborer to the information worker. Welcome to the Age of Information!
>
> A piechart of the workforce shows farmers at 3 percent; smokestackers at 20 percent; service people at 28 percent; information industries at 49 percent — statistics which do not show the dependence all sectors have on information processing. The new society will produce information the way the old one mass-produced cars. In 1950 we created 93,000 businesses a year. Today we invent over 600,000.
>
> The global village is here, wired with optic fiber, cabled from pole to pole and encased in satellites. The high-tech people of the Age of Information will need a Church that both appreciates the meaning of a high-tech life and responds to the *high-touch* needs of Catholics. In its community, structure and meaning, the Church already has a high-touch capability.
>
> The *community* includes the Church's friendship network as well as the music, art, ceremony, eloquence, ministry, esthetics, ascetics and mystery of liturgy. The structure of the Church is made clear by the descriptions of roles, rights and duties of all the members in an open and free-flowing society. The Church's *meaning system* is a response to questions about the meaning and purpose of life. Community, structure and meaning — kept alive and updated — is an excellent high-touch response to the needs of high-tech Catholics of the age of the chip.
>
> Images of the Church of Vatican I, the Church of Vatican II and the "Chip Church" all come to mind in viewing Pope John Paul II's

visit to Africa. Before him stand one million pre-industrial rural
Africans, eager to hear this Vatican II presidential and collegial
pope of the industrial age. Overhead a satellite from the chip culture
hums, taking signals and beaming this scene to anyone on earth
who cares to watch. Layers of culture come together in one quick
insight — the receding past, the insistent present, the crashing-into-
us future.

What does this picture of social movement mean for the sweep
of history as it influences the image of the pope, the progress of
theology and the development of ministry?[17]

Therefore, who can tell the extent of cultural adaptation the
Church may have to face in the future? Father Rahner goes so far as
to state that:

> The new Christians who were the simple appendages to an
> otherwise European and later North American Church are the
> reflection of the dramatic pluralism of cultures that may even
> challenge the identity of the Gospel as European and Western.[18]

The meaning of this leap to a "world Church" is graphically
shown in many of the documents of Vatican II. The Pastoral
Constitution on the Church in the Modern World, considered to be
the document for the whole Church, revealed, as never before, the
presence of the Third World as a vital aspect of the Church of the
future. The victory for the use of the vernacular in the Constitution
on the Sacred Liturgy, would not have been possible without the
influence of missionary and Eastern Rite bishops. The Declaration
on the Relationship of the Church to Non-Christian Religions
opened the way for a positive approach to the great religions of the
world. And finally, to emphasize again the development of
doctrine in this area, the Declaration on Religious Freedom clearly
renounced for all situations in the world the use of any force in
proclaiming the message of Christ that is not implied in the power
of the Gospel itself.

On several occasions Pope Paul VI mentioned that for the first time in history, all the peoples on earth and all the traditions of the Church were able to make their voices heard at the Second Vatican Council. It would be a pity if those words of his, spoken at the opening of the fourth session in 1965, were to be silenced at the grassroots of the Church of the future. Vatican II was indeed a pastoral Council because it was a gathering of pastors who came to Rome with the "sensus fidelium." It is important that the faithful they represented do not lose hope. The Church of the future must be a Church of hope. As Father Rahner put it:

> It understands itself as the sacrament of hope for the world, as the place, the sign, and tool of the Spirit of Jesus Christ who, according to the fourth gospel, tells us what is to come. [19]

Father Walter Kasper, whom I quoted earlier, emphasizes that the faithful should not be misled by what appears to be a temporary stagnation of the spirit of the Council. He feels that for the sake of the Church's future it would be fatal if this development were more than a temporary pause for breath to gather strength.

The present stagnation, according to Father Kasper, is a fear of the future that exists among conservatives as well as progressives. The former are unhappy because they think the Spirit should work only in the forms already known to them; the latter, only in the forms and tempo they expect. Both are shutting themselves off from the actual summons of the Spirit.

I would like to believe that the Second Vatican Council has an assured future and that it will condition the life of the Church for a long time to come. After all, it was a work of the Spirit, and the new Pentecost it generated, like the first, will need the prayers of all the People of God. The seeds were planted and if they are nourished we can say with our Lord:

> "I tell you, lift up your eyes and see how the fields are waiting for the harvest" (John 4:35).

FOOTNOTES

(For fuller citations of sources, please see the Bibliography)

1. *Council Daybook*, Vol. 1, p. 7.
2. *Origins* (NC Documentary News Service, Washington, D.C.), Dec. 19, 1985.
3. Abbott, pp. 10-11.
4. Rahner, *Concern for the Church*, p. 145.
5. Kasper, p. 207.
6. *Origins*, Dec. 19, 1985.
7. Kasper, p. 207.
8. Butler.
9. Rahner, *Theological Investigations*, Vol. 5, p. 253.
10. Boff, p. 3.
11. Congar, p. 31.
12. *Vatican II Revisited*, p. 327.
13. *Origins*, Sept. 18, 1986.
14. *Origins*, Dec. 19, 1985.
15. Congar, p. 25.
16. Ibid., p. 24.
17. McBride, pp. 162-163.
18. Rahner, *Concern for the Church*, p. 145.
19. Ibid.

Bibliography

Walter Abbott. *The Documents of Vatican II* (New York: America Press, 1966). All quotations from Vatican II documents are from this book.

_____. *Twelve Council Fathers* (New York: Macmillan Co., 1963).

Leonardo Boff. *Church: Charism and Power* (New York: Crossroad, 1985).

Bernard R. Bonnot. *Pope John XXIII: An Astute, Pastoral Leader* (Staten Island, NY: Alba House, 1979).

Christopher Butler. *The Theology of Vatican II* (Westminster, MD: Christian Classics, 1981).

Code of Canon Law (Washington, D.C.: CLSA, 1983).

Commentary on the Documents of Vatican II (Herbert Vorgrimler, gen. ed.) (New York: Herder and Herder, 5 Vols. 1967-1969).

Yves Congar. *Le Concile De Vatican II* (Paris: Beauchesne, 1984).

Council Daybook (Floyd Anderson, ed.) (Washington, D.C.: National Catholic Welfare Conference, 3 Vols. 1965).

Walter Kasper. *Jesus The Christ* (New York: Paulist Press, 1977).

Alfred McBride. *The Story of the Church* (Cincinnati: St. Anthony Messenger Press, 1983).

The Papal Encyclicals (Claudia Carlen, IHM, ed.) (Wilmington, NC: McGrath Pub. Co., Vol. 5, 1981).

Karl Rahner. *Concern For The Church* (New York: Crossroad, 1981).

_____. *Theological Investigations* (Baltimore: Helicon Press, Vol. 5, 1966).

Joseph Ratzinger. *Problems of the Church Today* (Washington, D.C.: National Conference of Catholic Bishops, 1976).

Xavier Rynne. *Letters From Vatican City* (New York: Farrar, Straus & Giroux, 1963). This volume is cited in the footnotes as Rynne.

_____. *The Second Session* (1964).

_____. *The Third Session* (1965).

_____. *The Fourth Session* (1966).

George Tavard. *The Pilgrim Church* (New York: Herder and Herder, 1967).

Vatican II Revisited (Minneapolis: Winston Press, 1986).

Antoine Wenger. *Vatican Council II: The First Session* (New York: Paulist Press, 1966).

Vincent A. Yzermans. *American Participation in the Second Vatican Council* (New York: Sheed and Ward, 1967).

Name Index

Abbott, Walter 41, 122
Adam, Karl 8
Ahern, Barnabas 8, 22, 78-81
Alfrink, Bernard 22, 43
Alter, Karl 137
Arrupe, Pedro 46

Balic, Karl 28
Baum, Gregory 8, 23, 32
Bea, Augustin 8, 41, 42, 75, 76, 106,
    108, 109, 115, 117-120, 122
Becker, Werner 108, 109
Bekkers, Willem 72
Bergin, Clifford 22, 133
Boff, Leonardo 171-173
Bouyer, Louis 8
Butler, Christopher 19, 20, 34, 46, 76-
    78, 170

Camara, Helder 145
Canestri, Giovanni 114
Capovilla, Loris 7
Carli, Luigi 46
Chenu, Marie Dominique 30, 31
Ciappi, Luigi 33
Coderre, Gerard 157, 158
Congar, Yves 6, 8, 23, 30-32,
    109, 148, 172, 176, 177
Conway, William 57
Cullmann, Oscar 110, 111
Cushing, Richard 121

Dearden, John 154, 156
de Lubac, Henri 28, 29
De Smedt, Emile 18, 43, 44, 51, 74,
    112, 128-131, 139

Diekmann, Godfrey 8, 23, 50
Doepfner, Julius 22, 42, 91, 92
D'Souza, Eugene 46
Dwyer, George 114, 115

Elchinger, Arthur 50, 51, 98, 99, 163

Falls, Thomas 91
Felici, Pericle 17, 18, 35, 36, 46, 47,
    133
Frings, Joseph 42, 45, 46
Frotz, Augustin 158

Garrone, Gabriel 46, 154
Geiselmann, Josef 8
Greco, Charles 96, 97
Green, Joseph 24
Guardini, Romano 8
Gueranger, Prosper 8, 9

Hallinan, Paul 68, 158-160
Hamer, Jerome 33
Hannan, Philip 46, 154
Haring, Bernard 33
Heenan, John 34, 152, 153
Helmsing, Charles 46
Higgins, George 23, 63, 107
Hooft, Vincent 8
Hooft, W. Visser't 10, 11
Howard, Joseph 22
Huergo, Alverno 33
Hume, Basil 166
Hurley, Dennis 57

Isaac, Jules 115, 116

John XXIII   ix-xii, 3, 4, 6-8, 10, 11, 13-15, 25-29, 32, 34-37, 39, 42, 46, 52, 53, 56, 61, 67, 74-77, 85, 97, 104, 106, 108-112, 115-117, 129, 130, 136, 139, 141-144, 146, 148, 151, 161, 163, 166-168, 173
John Paul II   xii, 61, 171-175, 177-179
Jungmann, Josef   8

Kasper, Walter   169, 170, 180
Kennedy, Eugene   93
Koenig, Franz   29
Küng, Hans   23, 27

Lagrange, Marie Joseph   8
Leahy, William   41
Leger, Paul   44, 45, 71, 114, 157
Leo XIII   xii, 114
Lercaro, Giacomo   45, 145, 146, 152, 153
Lienart, Achille   42, 45, 46
Ligutti, Luigi   23

McBride, Alfred   178, 179
McCann, Owen   100
McCool, Francis   22, 78
McGrath, Marcos   46, 99, 155, 173
McManus, Frederick   68
Maly, Eugene   23
Marcinkus, Paul   23
Marmion, Columba   8
Marty, Francis   57, 58, 86
Meyer, Albert   v, xii, 15, 18, 22-24, 42, 43, 45, 57, 70, 71, 74, 76, 78, 79, 86, 87, 99, 100, 121, 132-134, 136, 137, 140, 151, 152
Moehler, Charles   27
Moeller, Charles   143, 149
Murray, John Courtney   23, 31, 126-128, 131, 133, 139, 140

O'Brien, Elmer   8
O'Donnell, Cletus   22, 23, 43, 99, 133
Ottaviani, Alfredo   26, 28, 44, 45, 71, 138, 155

Paul VI   10, 33, 37, 40, 52, 58, 89-91, 100, 117, 119, 120, 125, 126, 133-136, 141, 144, 145, 149, 151, 152, 155, 156, 159, 161-163, 167, 168, 171, 172, 180
Pavan, Pietro   33
Philips, Georg   27
Pius XII   7, 9, 10, 25, 27, 28, 31-33, 38, 73, 77
Primeau, Ernest   23, 62, 63, 135

Quiroga y Palacios, Fernando   138

Rahner, Karl   27, 29, 30, 148, 168-170, 177, 179, 180
Ratzinger, Joseph   81
Ritter, Joseph   105, 114, 120, 121, 136
Rodrigues, Michael   118
Ruffini, Ernesto   7, 42, 77, 105, 106, 137, 138, 152
Rynne, Xavier   103, 112, 133, 151

Saigh, Maximos IV   44, 68-70, 113, 114, 119, 157
Schillebeeckx, Edward   30, 32, 33
Sidarouss, Stephanos I   119
Spellman, Francis   15, 31, 42, 43
Suenens, Leo   18, 32, 42, 43, 52, 55, 60, 99, 142-145, 147, 151, 156-158, 167, 168

Tappouni, Ignazio   105, 118
Tardini, Domenico   6, 7
Tavard, George   26, 27, 41, 75, 106
Thils, Gustav   27
Tisserant, Eugene   22, 44, 70, 89, 117, 132-135
Tromp, Sebastian   28

Wenger, Antoine   41, 144-146
Willebrands, Jan   28, 29
Wright, John   63, 64, 96, 97, 137

Yzermans, Vincent   42, 43